THE OTHER CHICAGO MOB

The True Story of

Gary Cohen, Man in Blue

Verne Elliot Glassman

GE Publications, LLC
2075 S. University Blvd
Ste. 241
Denver, CO 80210

The author and the publisher of *The Other Chicago Mob
The True Story of Gary Cohen, Man in Blue* make no claims
of absolute correctness of facts and accept no liability
for this literary work beyond the reasonable efforts that
have been undertaken to obtain news articles supporting
the main events of this story. This book is based on
the recollection and input of Gary Cohen and the
information included is from interviews with Mr. Cohen.

ISBN 978-0-9800949-1-6

Contact:
Sales Department
GE Publications, LLC
2075 S. University Blvd
Ste. 241
Denver, CO 80210
Phone: 303-517-0015
or e-mail: sales@gepub.com
www.gepub.com

Printed and bound in the United States of America

Library of Congress Cataloging-in-Publication Data
available from publisher

DEDICATION

Dedicated to the ladies in my life, Bonita and Avemaria, my girls Britt and Randi, and the thin Blue Line, who serve and Protect.

Gary Cohen

Dedicated to my late father, Alex, who encouraged writing and all things creative, and to every member of the United States Armed Forces who go in harm's way so that I may have the freedom to write. A final dedication to my Mother, Roslyn, a source of inspiration.

Verne Elliot Glassman

CONTENTS

I am a writer on many subjects, but I have to say none more interesting than helping to tell the story of Gary Cohen, a Chicago Cop. Gary and I are very much alike, and yet our backgrounds are quite different. Yet we have found so many levels of common interest and experience that this work has become both personal for both of us and also important in what it says. I will simply say this is a story that has not been told, period.

This tale is told essentially in episodes or vignettes by an individual who experienced more in 20 years on the force than any average 20 people can expect to know in a lifetime. It is also a story of strength and weakness, of flaws, of success and failure and ultimately of survival. Gary's story is unique. It is precisely spoken and historically accurate as only one recounted by a participant can be with in sardonic humor, gritty detail and unblinking honesty.

You will be transported to the City Streets of Chicago, to the Subway, to the '68 Convention, to shootings, violence and mayhem on a grand scale, and you will question how anyone could survive such circumstances. Gary, in looking back at his career (the first part of his career), was more a brute than a part time thief and more a part time opportunist than a dishonest cop. This may be picking at small points, but it is essential to understanding the growth and transition that took place in order to tell this story. A story of this sort is a journey from one place to another, from one point to another point. In the 20 years, the man who started the trip is not the same one who finished it; people mature and grow.

This is first person reporting of events that society has mostly chosen to sweep under the carpet and not acknowledge. This is the story of a Police Department rotten to its core, yet still dedicated to its city, the story of the last dictator of politics, of world events coming together in the 1968 Democratic Convention and how this event defines our country to this day. This story has been hidden, whispered about and roundly denied by those in position to be painted by its brush, but the time has come for one man to set the record straight.

Gary was a cop. He was a brutal man. He was an opportunist (part-time thief) in an organization of professional thieves, and yet he became so much more. The order of the day was to control by violence and coercion, but even with this, the "good guys" were vastly better than the "bad guys." The culture defined the times and the times defined how people behaved. There was the code of silence practiced at all levels of the Police Department, the need to put down pervasive violence in the streets, and to maintain or restore order. What is necessary one day may not look so pretty years later, but the code was not to talk, not to question and not to rat, just to fall in the long blue line and do what you see your peers do. The rule they lived by is summed up in a common saying among cops, "It is better to be judged by twelve than carried by six."

To try and change the system first required the desire to do so, but then also the means. It took years for the desire and the means and the opportunity to coincide and allow some of that change. Cities grow, Departments grow and people grow; we never remain the same. For better or worse, this is what being a cop in Chicago from 1966 to 1988 entailed. To wish for something different is pie in the sky.

Some chapters consist of vignettes of operations and police work told from the inside. Gritty and honest to a fault, they tell the larger story of how one man, a Department (to some degree) and a city redefined themselves and rose from the ashes to achieve something better. Other chapters describe how things worked (or didn't work), as well as those whom spoke of the inner struggle and the few people who helped in the journey.

It is said that to ignore the past is to relive the past. That is why this story is so important. People age and die, stories are lost, and pretty soon there is no first person account and only revisionist history. We can see this happening to this very day. The purpose of this book is not to seek atonement for past misdeeds, but rather to right a history long misrepresented and to set the record straight.

Read this book on any level you wish. The book stands as a testament to an individual whom I respect very much, but it goes well beyond that.

It details events that changed the world in '68, the transition of the Chicago Police Department from the Old West model to that of modern policing, and a city that needs to deal with its past so it can claim its future. There is no time like the present to take a hard look at what has been to help determine what may be. In this regard, I would ask: How can a flawed and diseased city hope for better without first admitting to its past? Read the papers and you will find many of the same problems existing today that are described 40 years ago and, in fact, the names have hardly changed.

One last thing to consider as you read this history told by a key participant: How is it that an intelligent person from a good home with values can also be the voice of 20 years of criminal activity, brutality and excess? How can one person have gravitated to characters who would later be shown to be mass murderers and felons without conscience or equal? The answer may require a professional to decipher, but for me it's simple. Gary is a very intelligent, charismatic person. The most heinous criminals and psychopaths are also often charming and charismatic people who attract and con others. Magnets either attract or repel. In our true story, more often than not it's the attraction of strong and colorful personalities that help the real players stand out. We are talking about characters larger than life, the rock stars and the royalty of the nether world of cops and robbers, protectors and predators. This is a colorful tapestry of almost mythological proportions. The only surprise is that it is real; the stories told actually happened and these people played the parts for real—and just as real were the consequences.

Please enjoy *The Other Chicago Mob.* If it strikes a responsive chord, I encourage you to study further on this subject and to be open to the real history, over 40 years old and just now starting to be told.

INTRODUCTION

I will introduce myself more formally a little later in this book, but for now let's just say my name is Gary Cohen, and I was a Jewish Chicago cop from 1966 to 1988. I was also a brute, a witness to history, "and an "opportunist", which is to say a part-time thief. This is my story, but also the story of Chicago and its Police Department, and as it happens, the story of when the United States made an abrupt and violent turn from the status quo to the future. Let me also say I am being as honest as I can in this telling and have not consciously subverted or changed any event to make myself or others look better than we were. So, for better or worse, this is unvarnished history reported first-hand and without reservation on my part.

This is not the first time some of the larger events written here have been presented, but to the best of my knowledge, this book is unique in that the information reported is firsthand. I witnessed the events discussed and did not learn of the details second or thirdhand or from other published reports or descriptions. If I said it happened a certain way, it happened that certain way according to my eyes and memory, having participated directly in the action described. Very limited "creative modification" has been sparingly used to cut through the clutter and still not lose the essence of events. In no chapter have events been made up or fictionalized. I am the first to admit that historical events are open to wide interpretation, but as in court proceedings, particular weight and credibility is given to eyewitness accounts and that is what I am giving you.

I have left out items that can cause me or others real legal jeopardy, but do not alter events to make a point or to enhance drama. This is like no police story ever told, and even that speaks to decades-old efforts to cover up or subvert the truth. I hope my honesty in these pages, (your call since I am partially dishonest) may set the record straight or at least encourage greater inspection and scrutiny of those important years.

Chicago from 1966 to 1988 was a treasure trove of humor, violence and world-changing events. What must be not missed, however, is the underlying system or "machine" that allows such things to flourish. While most of my vignettes can stand by themselves, they more correctly belong in the sequence of events that later made history and as such are the symptoms of a dysfunctional system and city. The real disease was (and perhaps still is) the City Government, the Department, and the temptations. Take note that no serious attempt has ever been made to correct the disease. All efforts are always directed toward the symptoms.

Chapter 1

In 1970 (four years after I started the job) I was assigned to a Special Unit, a task force with the sole purpose of reclaiming the Subway System (the El) from the thugs and making it safe for the riders once again. The background to this is that several gangs had staked out the "El" by subway stops, and each had their own to exploit. In the process, several prominent Chicagoans, including a few high profile reporters, were mugged, robbed and severely beaten on the "EL". Mayor Daley would have none of that, so the word came down as if from on high to take back our subways and the only thing that would count would be results; methods were of little concern to City Hall. Do it and do it now.

Up to this point, the Transportation Police were more like Black Sheep Goofballs than an elite police unit. Most assigned to the caverns were those under investigation, about to be indicted, malcontents or dead wood; this was not a career- making or career - enhancing assignment. I was sent there to right some disciplinary wrong (I wish I could be more specific, but there were so many of them), and my sole duty was to accompany one of the other "Transportation Cops" to make sure he didn't step on the "third rail." The third rail was the one carrying the current and to touch it meant to die. It was actually a fairly popular way to buy the farm, though somehow its charm was always lost on me. When the call from City Hall came down, it was decided that of the 260 or so officers who made up this unit, a small subset would be recruited to work the Subway Robbery Task Force, so we were the dirty half dozen of the Chicago Police Department. We may have been misfits but we were also the best of the best at "unconventional police work," and this was to get as unconventional as it comes.

Ours was an elite team made up of six officers. You might say it takes a thief to catch a thief and I couldn't disagree, but in point of fact we were more like actors playing a role, a part we were very good at. In later years, one of our team would find himself in the witness protection program (for all the wrong reasons) and another would become an Alderman from the 40th Ward. Still another, our designated target, referred to in the papers as the "Man With the Golden Watch," was almost pathological and, though physically small, was the most violent and dangerous member of our unit. We were an eclectic group of hard-nosed professionals and we liked what we did; that this also happened to correspond to our assigned duties on the force was a bonus.

We let our beards grow, wore civies, and each night would go down into the system, the complex of stations. We would use a decoy, a member of the team dressed up a little differently each night, who would act wasted. For realism he usually was three sheets, but then a sober person would never let himself be mugged literally hundreds of times without some reinforcement (not referring to backup in this case). This "decoy" had to be unarmed and absolutely realistic, both in action and odor. Over the many months we worked the detail, he (always the same guy played victim, as the rest of us were just a bit smarter) ended up frequenting Chicago's Henrotin Hospital with contusions, concussions and knife wounds, not a real good job as far as retirement is concerned. We nabbed a few hundred arrests and shot and killed a handful (which also took them off the mean streets).

We met well after dark, around 12:30 a.m., sometimes later, and gathered on a lower platform. I would walk down the flights of concrete stairs and sidestep the puddles. Businessmen with folded newspapers would hurry on by not looking to the right or left, and the occasional housewife caught out late shopping would rush along, not making eye contact, knowing the danger she was in. I would walk up to my group from the Tactical Unit, five men in different dress, huddled in a semicircle under a light to the edge of the landing. Two or three Uniformed Police were also there. As I join the group someone hands me a cup of coffee; one of the guys says his wife sent along a thermos so he wouldn't catch cold down there, like that's the least of anyone's worries. Some are smoking, wearing worn gloves with the fingers missing. Finally Humphrey says "Guys, I ain't getting any younger so what say we set up shop?" We all nod and trudge off. Down more stairs to the platform and the turnstyles; most of the guys just hop over them and continue on the other side. We get to the platform and it is now pretty deserted.

The uniforms go off behind some columns leading up to the cathedral ceiling and the rest of us assume our positions. Humphrey takes a swig from his flask and then splashes some of the booze over his worn, torn jacket and starts to wander back and forth on the edge of the platform. Me and Art sit by the mildewed concrete wall and pull our knees up and slump our heads down. It is now 1:15 a.m. and we are officially open for business. The yellow overhead light casts shadows and we hear the sound of distant trains in the tunnel. Over the PA system it's announced, "B train arriving Washington Street, B train arriving Washington Street." The train light appears far up the tunnel. The sound increases and the overhead lights flicker. The train screeches to a halt and the doors open, nobody gets on or off. The doors close and the train moves off.

Someone whispers, "Heads up, we got customers." From up the platform come two scummy looking guys, one black, one white. Both are wearing oversized jackets and one has a pull-over cap and the other a baseball hat and both are smoking. Humphrey pulls his golden watch and shakes it and looks down and puts it away and keeps walking, looking down. The two thugs come up to him and one says, "Hey guy, got the time?" Humphrey says nothing. The other punk says, "Man, my friend asked you for the fucking time," and slugs our decoy in the face and down he goes and lays there. One of the fucks leans down to roll Humphrey when out from under his coat Humphrey takes a length of lead pipe and smashes it with all his might into the guy's ankle, which breaks with the sound of a dry branch and he goes down with a piercing scream. As Humphrey regains his feet (he is tougher than he let on, but still has blood coming from his nose), Art and I run up and slug the other guy and bring him to his hands and knees, blood and saliva flowing from his mouth and nose. Humphrey takes the first guy's hair in his left hand pulls his head back and gives him a savage short punch to the bridge of the nose. Blood shoots out of his face and he falls back unconscious, his head making a wet sound as it hits the concrete. I lean over the second guy and using a sap, a leather pouch filled with lead shot, smash him across the back of the head. His scalp opens up clear to the bone. Blood is everywhere and he falls on his face. One of the other guys says, "Gary, you know if you use a sap you are going to split the fuck's head open," and I answer, "Yeah, I know."

Two of the Uniforms come up and cuff the crooks and drag them off for the hospital and booking. This repeats itself a few more times. That early morning and around 4:00 a.m. Humphrey says, "Hell, guy's, I think we bagged our quota for the good Mayor so let's call it a night. Anyone care for some coffee or breakfast?" We collect our shit and climb the stairs back to street level.

In case anyone questions why we employed overwhelming force to take down the crooks, it's because you never know when they are armed and our decoy isn't, so there is no nice way to ask these fucks to "please" stop their assault while we arrest them.

The "EL" was no place for wimps or the timid after dark or in the small hours but for us it was easy hunting. This was before the days of entrapment and bleeding heart concern for the welfare and treatment of the misunderstood pathological scum we sought, so our hand was pretty free to do as we wished as long as it got results. Anyway, after many weeks of this stuff it started to get just a little boring, each night the same with only the location changing. Then inspiration struck.

We were working the entertainment district (theaters, not the other type of entertainment), and while setting up in the late afternoon found a theatrical supply house open just down the block. Not wanting simply another night of routine violence and gratuitous mayhem we chipped in and rented a Superman costume. We then descended into the bowels of the system. As we go lower and lower, we start to smell that musky dampness like an old basement and the walls are almost slimy. Off to the side of the platform we found a very heavy metal gate, seven feet high and maybe five feet wide, that protected tools and other heavy equipment in an access alcove adjacent to the station platform. This thing weighed a few hundred pounds, but we were able to take out the holding pins and our skeleton key (a universal key) worked on the lock. We had by this time dressed up our largest team member, clean shaven, square jawed and muscular (a onetime college football player, defensive end) and put him in the enclosure with a police radio. It was now late at night, actually around 1:00 a.m. the next morning, and we decided to open shop and see what scum slithered by.

So here we are, our all too real plastered decoy with a crumpled business suit on, staggering up and down the platform, dim yellow lights adding a good mood, me and a couple others in plainclothes and another two or three guys in their Blues who were assigned to back up our force hiding in the shadows. We are in concealment when two guys come up the platform and do what is typically done, which is to ask the drunk for some change or a light. At this time they punch the guy, our guy, square in the gut and he goes down like a big sack of garbage. The two suspects (what we liked to call them when talking to reporters, otherwise we called them motherfuckers, as in, "Hey, you two suspects, back away from the drunk and put your hands behind your heads"(it has a certain ring to it). The lowlife's had knelt down to roll our guy when there is this ungodly crash from down the platform that echoes up and down the tunnel, and out steps Superman, standing under a harsh high intensity light that marked the end of the access way, his face and body cut by angular shadows. Our two scumbags look up with alarm and see our guy standing there in all his glory, hands on hips, and he walks slowly over to them. He puts a massive paw on each of their shoulders and pulls them up, almost off the ground.

Our guy is maybe 6' 6" and rock solid, and there he is with each mighty hand on the bad guy's shoulders. The thugs both yell at the same time, "Superman, what the fuck are you doin' here, man?" Our guy answers, "The Chicago Police Force and Mayor Daley asked that I come down from Metropolis and lend a hand with making the subway safe once again for the fine citizens of Chicago, and you two evildoers are under arrest for assaulting and attempting to rob this good citizen here. Officers, take them away!" Out from the shadows behind the pillars come a couple of District Cops and they cuff the guys and start to lead them off. One of the motherfuckers, "suspects" turns his head as he climbs the concrete stairs and says, "Hey Superman, say it ain't so, bro, say it ain't so."

These guys are taken down to the station for booking and we show up a short time later for reports and to check out. The Sergeant is standing facing these same two guys when they relate their story about Superman and he hauls back and back hands them both across the face, pretty damn hard, knocking the snot out of both of them. "Don't give me that shit, you scumbags," he hollers, spit flying from his mouth, and walks away. He meets us in the hall and says, "Hey, guys, anything you want to fill me in on?" to which we shake our heads and just mumble, "Ah-no."

Two weeks pass and these same two guys are being arraigned in court and of course we are all there. Superman is now dressed in a very nice gray business suit and has on plain black glasses and a conservative gray hat. These guys keep looking over at him nervously, can't take their eyes off him actually. He doesn't look directly at them, but makes notes in his small reporter's pad and every so often pushes his glasses back off his nose with a finger to the middle of the nosepiece. A lock of jet black hair keeps slipping from under his hat and he also takes a moment to push it back, only to have it slip out again. His square jaw doesn't move. Actually, the only part of his face that shows any life are his eyes, which take in everything and miss nothing. Obviously, he is a reporter and a man of, well, steel.

"All rise, the Honorable Judge So and So is taking the bench," followed by a loud gavel hit and "Court is now is session, please take your seats; Bailiff, first case." "Your Honor, the State of Illinois against so and so, for aggravated assault and attempted robbery." "How do you plead?" "Ahh, ahh, not guilty, your Honor." They keep looking over at Clark Kent instead of the Judge. The Judge looks up from his papers and says sharply, "what are you guys looking at" and they answer, "Superman, Sir, ah we mean Clark Kent!" The Judge puts the papers down and stares right through these two crooks as if looks could kill. He says, with an irritated, barely controlled loud voice, "I am sending you two over to County for a complete mental evaluation and suggest you not try to play fast with this court when this comes to trial. Take them away!"

This hits the papers with some particularly penetrating comments from the Chicago Sun- Times about how Chicago's finest needed outside help from Metropolis to do their jobs. The *Chicago Magazine* (similar to the *New Yorker*) did a 12 page spread on this in even greater detail. The next day, our unit was broken up and we were scattered all over the police map, never to work together again.

Probably best they broke us up when they did since we had a bear costume on reserve for the next week.

It's my understanding Superman returned to Metropolis soon after, his job done and mass transit once again safe for Chicagoans. Thank you, Man of Steel for making, and saving our day. You live in our hearts and added just that little extra measure to crime fighting lore in the Windy City.

Sometimes you just need Superman to get the job done right.

As a side note to underscore the absurdity of this world we worked in, one day a new sergeant was assigned to our unit in some sort of management role, but he wanted to do the deed at least once so he could say he'd earned his bones. Since our Man with the Golden Watch (Humphrey) was still in the hospital that night we had this fresh face play the mark. One absolute rule of our road is that the decoy should never be armed, but I guess that didn't apply to our new guy. We set up as usual and as always a couple of vermin come out of the shadows and approach our guy. I don't know what spooked our decoy but he pulls out a .38 Special snub nose revolver and, without a word being spoken shoots the guy nearest him in the chest, square in the chest. This shit's breast bone becomes a gushing hole and a large section of his back lifts off and he falls, just like he was a puppet and someone instantly cut all his strings. He lands on the concrete with a wet sounding thud, his face up. His heart is beating and arterial blood from his chest pulsates the blood in a mini-fountain from the hole. You should have seen the look on the other guy's face; it's not nice to learn in an instant that you are the hunted and no longer the hunter. We come out and secured the fuckup that is still standing and then search the new road kill, well almost killed. It was early in the evening so he didn't have any cash on him, but he did have a nasty, dirty knife in his pants. We put that aside and arranged to transport the standing one to the lockup. Our new fuck up is now really worried, concerned that this may not be viewed as a "Good-shooting". This nobrains wonder calls one of our guys over and has him bring him the knife we just took off the wounded guy. The shooter tells one of our guys to take the knife and to stab him in the arm, so it looks like he was defending himself. We could care less one way or another, so our guy, without so much as a "This will hurt," shoves this shiv halfway into the fellow's arm. Never did see anyone so happy to be knifed in my life; also we never saw him again, which was fine by me. We lost perfectly good leadership and the city found a new hero. Damn near perfect.

We started getting press coverage every day, sort of like the vigilante patrol, and the public just ate this up. Our mark, our Man with the Golden-Watch was very popular. Humphrey was known by the big, cheap gold watch. We were hardly even set up when these mopes come up to him and say, "Hey man, like we know this is a fuckin setup, but hand over that fuckin watch" and they were arrested. We also worked on the subways and the regular riders, on seeing us, would burst into applause and give words of encouragement. We were actually too successful, so even without Superman's help we knew our days were numbered.

I will reveal a small secret about this story and here it is; it's for real. Without embellishment, this is how it went down; Superman was in fact our largest team member and usually carried a bag of makeup and prosthetics and amassed one of the most impressive records in the Department. Our Mark, James Humphrey, for some reason, relished being beat upon and was pound for pound the strongest, meanest member of the team, a mean-spirited killer with a hair trigger but otherwise an all round nice guy. Throughout his career our man, the Man with the Golden Watch, sought out danger and confrontation and never came in second in a fight. He later would go over lock, stock, and barrel to the dark side and became a full-time hood. I, being the youngest, was a boy with a bunch of neat toys, and I liked to play rough and I never, ever shared.

CALL OF THE DARK SIDE

Chapter 2

Jim Humphrey, what really happened to you, man? I first worked with Jim when I started on the Mass Transit Team and spent three years with him. Jim Humphrey was/is a man so unique that by court order the mold used to make him was broken in five pieces; four were sent to the four corners of the compass and the fifth shot into the sun.

He's the one and only. He and I were sort of the same, yet we came from two very different worlds. He was poor Irish from a broken home, a streetwise kid who spent every waking moment trying to overcome that fact. While he had the same opportunities for enrichment as the rest of us in those days, it was never enough for him; he was always seeking the gold ring. He was charismatic, handsome and disarmingly charming and that was his ticket to the show. He could fool anyone, including me. He was the kind of person you gravitate to; bigger than life and a thespian at heart. This served him well and helped make him one of Chicago's most famous and decorated police officers, a legend and a myth. He always needed to outdo himself and in his mind it was never good enough to talk the talk, he had to always walk the walk.

He could be a decent friend, but he could also be your absolute worst enemy. Jim was a chameleon and could change character quicker than I could change clothes. In an instant he could go from easy going affable to a frenzied demon and the trip wire was usually a mystery. Early on I had occasion to pull him off a man he was beating to death on a subway platform. James stood up, grabbed my shirt and backing me into a column said, "Don't you ever, ever interfere with me again when I am doing something." And he returned to beating the crap out of the fuck on the ground. I am perhaps a third larger and taller than he, but he slammed me into that column like I was a 90 pound Girl Scout. I told him then that this wouldn't work for me, that if we were to work together he had to respect my opinion on what would keep us out of trouble and that he needed to heed that advice when given; I was on his side. That arrangement worked, and I believe to this day I was perhaps the only person able to redirect Jim's anger when he was in a full rage.

Jim, from a previous assignment, had decent history with the new Commanding Officer who would later set up the Tactical Unit (Decoy Team). He came to me one day and said he had inside information that this decoy team was going to be established and then tried at every opportunity to convince me to join him. I was not very interested, as my sole ambition at that time was to get out of Mass Transit and return to mainline uniformed police work. I simply wasn't ready to put my butt on the line on bullshit; I was more of a mind to overcome my previous history with the Department and coast to retirement. That was not meant to be. Jim was quite the salesman and would point out the advantages of working plainclothes: your own hours, dress and look as you wish and are free from supervision. After a time this began to sound pretty good to me. While Jim dressed and played the part of a drunk, I on the other hand dressed as I wished and that entailed long hair, a beard and youthful clothes: In this I dressed on duty as I liked to dress when off. So finally I agreed and joined him and a few like-minded cops with the Mass Transit Tactical Unit. This worked for me but really worked for Jim; he was his own press secretary and became a media star. We each had to undergo baptism by fire by being the decoy and mine came early on: From that day forward, I was a full fledged member of the team. Jim trusted his life to me and my fellow undercover officers and was never armed, though he still was seriously hurt on numerous occasions. His exploits were documented almost daily by Chicago area newspapers. He created his own monster and whether or not his was Dr. Jekyll and Mr. Hyde before the Tactical Unit, by the time we were done he had a duel personality. You never knew with Jim which one you would get, though he was promoted to the rank of Detective while still on the team and this just fed into his visions of grandeur. We worked with a free hand employing our tactics, the violence was concidered the means to the end, and we were given a bye, so we had little reason to fear retribution. We were doing the job of vigilante but with a badge and it suited the city and the population; we were exactly what the doctor ordered (or the Mayor actually). The once crime ridden Mass Transit System, a long-time bastion of mayhem and violence, had became a safer place. Any man with a beard or old coat could be an undercover officer. We brought peace to the system by projecting over-whelming violence against the perpetrators of crime and terrorism.

Jim was a man before his time and believed in equal opportunity; he would beat the crap out of anyone, for any reason, but he also was willing to take as well as give. He was our designated "vic-tim" in mass transit stings and would be beaten and savaged. This went on for around three years and I was always there to back him up when things went sour. What is important is that you watch each other's six, and even my wife appreciated his focus on my safety. When push comes to shove, being a per-son you can depend on is much more important to a fellow cop than character and he was always that go-to guy. At the time of one our shootings (With one offender already shot to death), it was Jim who, with blood lust, said to our Sergeant and those pres-ent that he was going to kill the other gang members still seated in the back seat of their car. It was just fortunate that I was able to reason with him and talk him out of this course of action. He would have shot and killed all the others and no one would have interfered; that's just how it was. Jim felt that he was omnipotent and above reproach and anything he did would only go to enhance his growing reputation, but in fact he was more a loose cannon that could hurt or kill innocent people as well as those deserving. He was a sociopath, but he was Chicago's sociopath so that sort of made it all right.

After our Mass Transit Decoy Unit was broken up, we went our different ways. Jim stated in a newspaper article of the day that he felt disillusioned upon going back into uniform and felt both unappreciated and used and subsequently quit the Department. He opened a hot dog stand, which failed, and then became a glazier. We saw each other on occasion and he always had a scheme for enrichment, but nothing concrete.

Then I read in the papers of Jim's involvement in front page crime. This was all the more shocking to the city due to his larger than life press while on the force and to his new role as a cold blooded mass murderer. On reflection, it was no surprise to those who knew him, but it was still a fall from grace of Olympian proportions. Along the line he lost track of good and evil and started to work across the grain. He teamed up with Jack Farmer, who was the leader of a gang of vicious thugs and killers. They were involved in extortion, break-ins, narcotics, strong arm and murder. In fact, what he did was to try and make his fortune doing something he was good at. Though it was not the Chicago Police Department that brought him down, it was the Feds.

Jim was indicted for around 17 counts of criminal activity, but then he simply vanished. Pouf, and he was gone without a trace. Since it is physically impossible to fall off the planet, the only thing that comes to mind is Witness Protection, but that is purely speculation. He may have been murdered since he crossed swords with organized crime by targeting some of their business when he was freelancing. Or it could have been any number of other questionable characters he brutalized in his long career. Probably we will never know. If he was killed, it never made the news.

Jim Humphrey was famous and lauded in print and TV when he worked Mass Transit as the Man with the Golden Watch. This was great press, but he will always be known and remembered for being infamous as one of Chicago's most violent and prolific killers who played both sides of the track. He holds the unique distinction of being one of the most notorious members of Chicago's other "Mob," the Chicago Police Department.

Jim, if you happen to read this know you are one of a kind among those I have known and I appreciate your saving my ass on many occasions. As to what you did after we parted company, let others pass judgment. I hope you have finally found some peace from the demons that always seemed to haunt you.

Chapter 3

Around three months into the job I was assigned to the Paddy Wagon. This was
very unusual since the Wagon was a "choice" assignment reserved for the older cops as a reward for
all their "hard work." Maybe it was a test to see
how I would handle the realities of the job, but this
is how that first day or evening went. I joined my
partner, Eddie Cash, for the midnight run. I am all
spit and polish and he is this rather sloppy giant of
an Irishman with hands the size of hams, and he was
wasted before we ever left the station.

The first thing he says to me is, "Kid, just sit
there and shut up,"—and this before I said anything.
Off we go and after a few minutes we pull off the
road to the back of some Hillbilly Bar off Wilson
Avenue and he honks once. A bartender comes out
and hands him a shot of Jim Beam. The bartender
says, "Hey, what about the kid?" and he answers,
"Na, he is new on the job and besides he ain't old
enough,to drink." I am sitting there looking straight
ahead and can't believe what I am hearing. We pull
away and five minutes later this repeats at another
bar. From there we start driving aimlessly around
in the Wagon when suddenly he slams on the brakes
and jumps out. He rushes up to this drunk and slaps
the shit out of him and steals what money he has,
maybe three bucks. He gets back into the wagon
and he tells me to hold the money, it's "Your job."

We go a little further, driving up alleys and down back streets when again we hit the brakes and he jumps out and again smashes some drunk and relieves him of four or five bucks. Gets back in and hands me the money. This repeats itself maybe ten times that first night and I can't believe what is happening. I am fresh out of the Academy and we are committing multiple armed robberies and this for maybe a total of 15 or 20 dollars and a few cents.

We continue to drive when all of a sudden he sees a car going the opposite direction and weaving. We do a 180 and hit the lights and siren. The car won't stop and we are chasing him in our truck (Wagon). Finally we pull up alongside and crash into the side of this guy's car, sending him flying over the curb and into a wall. Cash jumps out of the Wagon and rushes the driver, pulls open the door, drags him out like a rag doll and slaps him across the face with his massive paw. This guy had a knit hat on, pulled halfway over his face and I saw the hat fly off and for a moment thought it was the guy's head. The fellow is dragged to the back of the Wagon, the door opens and both he and my partner go into the back. I hear all sorts of thuds and sounds and the wagon is shaking and rocking like a small boat in a storm. Finally, my partner comes back to the cab and says, "Well, we can get five bucks from this fucker." I said, "Five bucks, to get off a DUI (47UART)!" My partner said "right" and goes back to the fellow in the rear and I hear more smashing and thrashing. Back he comes and says, "We're going into the station. Call for an Evidence Tech to meet us for the Breathalyzer at the 20th District."

We get there with me being the only sober one in the bunch and beat the tech by a couple of minutes. We go to an interrogation room and then the tech walks in and immediately asks "Who do I give the test to?" At this, our drunk "Client" picks up the recording device and smashes it against the wall and screams, "I want to see the Captain, this guy is drunker than I am!" The Captain comes over to see what the fuss is about, surveys the situation, says a few social howdy do's and tells the drunk to take a hike.

After my shift and after being party to ten or more armed robberies and assault of a prisoner in custody, I go home. Because my Dad had passed away just a short time before, my Mom was staying with me. She says in typical Jewish mother style voice, "And how was your first day?" I answered with tears streaming down my face, "Mom, don't ask."

The next day, I went into see the Captain and said, "I don't think I can work with Eddie any more." He said with a twinkle in his eye, "That's Okay, kid; it was just your turn in the barrel."

Chapter 4

The young don't consider death and the old can't think of much else, and maybe that is how it should be.

Some days stand out, the special ones you enjoy most, the ones where you cheat death. Some argue that you never hear the shot that kills you, but then you know it will be something. So who cares, really, who cares?

Personally, I just never gave it that much thought. On the force we were provided bullet-proof vests and at some point were required to wear them. I rarely did. Some people foolishly elect to never use seat belts; some cops never wear their vests.

I have been part of many major police operations, some involving other agencies. The planning starts early and is intensive. G-2 intelligence is disseminated, the site surveiled, the players identified, routes laid out and communication calls rehearsed. Raids are scripted like football. This is how it went on one typical raid.

The sun was going down, and the police teams take to their various vehicles, guns are charged and game faces put in place.

We leave the station and travel the darkening streets. At a designated point, our cars and trucks disperse and go in their prescribed routes. As we approach the scene in the warehouse district, we kill the lights and slow to a crawl. Around half a block away we stop and dismount, continuing on foot in case there is a lookout posted.

No night vision or other fancy electronics back then. Just you, your gun(s) and the sense that your team is around you. You approach the target and hug the wall, but it is getting quite dark and uncomfortably cold. Fingers are getting a little numb and so is your nose. Your nose starts to run, but you can't dab it, can't blow it, so you let it run. Your eyes dart around, and you move from one deep shadow to another. Various loading dock lights have come on, and a dirty yellow cast is thrown on everything. Distance is hard to gauge, and your eyes want to play tricks on you.

Just ahead is where you think you are supposed to be. Off on the right flank are some big industrial doors, but you have lost contact with most of your team and nothing looks like the black and white photos you viewed at the staging area. You continue on in dead silence. Finally, you decide to stop by a dumpster and just hope you are close to where you are to be. At precisely 11:17 there are a series of pops and the sound of breaking glass. Tear gas wafts here and there, stinging eyes and tongue. All is silent as the large door and the smaller door beside it open, and figures can be seen. My badge is displayed and I have my Smith and Wesson .41Mag out and some cotton in my ears just in case, when unexpectedly a shot is fired by someone, somewhere. Instantly all the planning goes out the window and guns go off all around you.

Figures are seen running and moving and you move also. Keeping low, you scurry around some crates and almost stumble in a hole in the concrete. You hear a shot somewhere up ahead, the whine of bullets hitting off of brick and concrete, yells, screams. This is a complete fur ball and everybody is shooting everywhere, you included. There is a flash forward of where you are and you fire at it and scoot to the right. You fire again. Shotguns, semi automatic weapons, pistols, automatics, all firing in staccato bursts.

Most gun fights seem to last hours, but rarely are more than three or four minutes. Time condenses and your focus is entirely on what is happening around you. Most exchanges of gunfire also happen within a distance of ten feet or less, and it's react, fire, react, crouch, fire, react, duck, yell, fire, run.

Afterward, you hear that for all the shots fired, only four bad guys were hit, one killed and one of the cops from another Unit was badly injured. Everyone had bruises, cuts, bumps and throbbing headaches. In those days no one did forensics, so no little yellow cones by the empty brass, no idea who shot whom, if the cop was hit by friendly fire or not. It was chaos, a fog, the smell of cordite in the air and an artificial low cloud from all the gunfire. When the firing stops one of the first things you hear are the stray cats screams and dogs barking out of fear or panic and this can go on for some time. As for the scene, no attempt will be made to make sense of it before sunup, and even then no one is particularly interested.

We got some bad guys, they got some good guys, and nobody knew what the fuck had happened. It would remain that way. Except that we rode home in the cars and trucks that brought us, this could have been the old west and little would have been different.

You know how when you go to an auto race you really, deep down want to see the crashes, the mayhem, the screaming of torn metal and the smell of hot oil and exhaust? People do die in such races.

People die doing what we did tonight, but then I know you don't get out of life alive so I don't wear a vest. If it's my time, then it's my time.

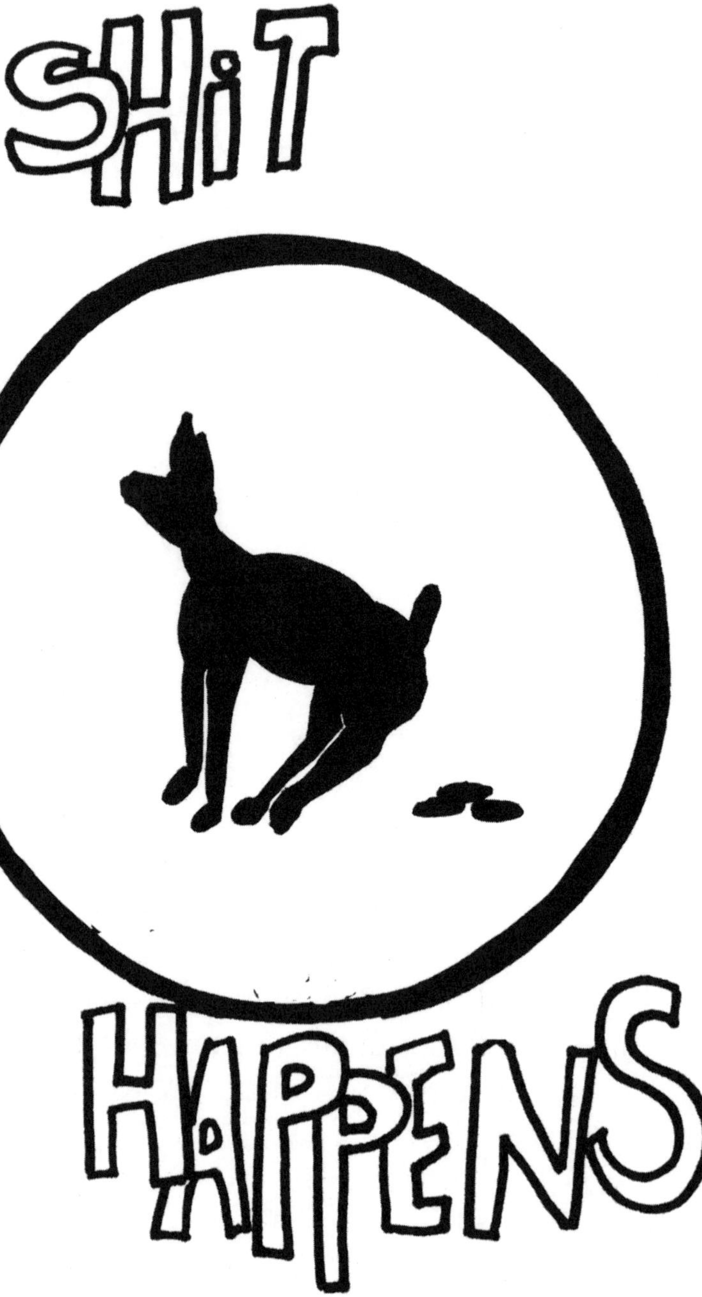
SHIT
HAPPENS

Chapter 5

I will take responsibility for my actions, but sometimes it's honestly not my fault; case in point.

For this episode you will need to pay close attention and follow the bouncing ball. A one and a two and a.............

Fairly early on in my career, I was the same devilishly handsome fellow you see today, but with thick hair and a little less baggage. I was really enjoying life and then, well ...

I was having dinner at a female acquaintance's apartment one evening and we were about to enjoy dessert when there is a loud knock on the door. This was an old three-story brownstone with a vacant lot next door where people parked. Spaces were not assigned, but were paid for by the renters. I was told just to park anywhere by the host's parking space. There is a pounding at the front door, and I rise to answer it, but the door bursts open and this guy, a drunk fellow, pushes his way into the apartment. He is loud and belligerent and shoves me, almost spitting in my face, wanting to know who I am and who parked in his space. His language was less than special as he insisted on calling me a Hippie Motherfucker. The discussion moves to the hall and this fellow takes a roundhouse swing at me, to which I answer with a short jab to his kidney area, and he goes down faster than the Titanic. He bounces right up and says he is calling the police, to which I responded, "Guy, you are really in luck. I am the police, so what can I do for you?" With this communicated, it is obvious the dialogue is over, as he turns and I advise him he is under arrest for assault. I call in for a pickup, and he is transported. There was a reason for my madness as anytime physical alterations are done to an individual by a cop an arrest is the best way to "cover your ass" and man did I ever need CYA.

A few days later, I pick up the daily paper and Mike Royko has a lead column with a story about this takedown, which happened not at a boxing match, not at a hockey game, not on a football field, but at the hands, the deadly hands of one of Chicago's finest hippie cops. It is now apparent that one punch has become the punch heard round the city and is a heater case. Upon arriving at the station, I am told by my Sergeant that I have a call waiting It is Mike Royko (Lead columnist for the *Chicago Daily News*.) He says he wants my comment on the story just written and I say, "It's a little late for that, so all I can offer you, and feel free to print this, FUCK YOU." Several other news articles on the vicious attack appeared, led by the victim (an Ex IRS Agent and current insurance agent to the newspaper; I sure knew how to pick them) who is now recovering at the hospital after having his spleen removed and who, by the way, was listed in serious condition. Through the agent's clout and connections, he had gotten a bench warrant from a sit-

ting judge in Criminal Court for aggravated battery.
Let's just say this is a serious deal and the ultimate
consequence could be prison time.

I went to court a few days later as one of the
guys I had arrested for trying to kill me was being
sentenced. When I got there I asked which court
room I should report to. The guy on duty just shook
his head and said Court Rooms B and C. "B and
C," I replied. "Yeh, the sentencing of your pinch is
in Court Room B and you are being indicted at the
same time in Court Room C." All I could think to
say was "Oh, well thanks." Since this was a first.

The arrest (mine) was served at my station,
and I was printed and photographed, in full uniform, and posted a $25 bond. The result was that
I was bounced from the elite Tactical Unit and put
in a squad car. My immediate concern was in find-
ing and enlisting the aid of a top criminal lawyer
in Chicago. Other than that, it was my intention to
keep so low a profile that an ant would look like
an elephant to me—that low. After interviewing a
number of top attorneys and with the input of other
cops, I found this whiz kid ex-prosecutor who was
now a defense attorney in private practice and was
high profile with many Mob clients. When I went
up to his office, I found myself sitting in the waiting room across from a distinguished looking el-
derly gentlemen, who struck up a conversation with
me. He seemed to know who I was and the basics
of my problem. My attorney and his partner came
out of his office and we were introduced. The el-

derly gentleman turned out to be Jackie Cerone, aka Jackie the Lackie, one of the heads of the Chicago Mob. He comes over and shakes my hand and says, "Good luck, kid." He goes into his attorney's office, and I go into mine.

We go to the preliminary hearing. This in itself is good fortune and due to my attorney's connections it did not go directly to the Grand Jury. At the hearing, my witness, my first-time date who was a school teacher as prim and proper as can be, said, "She was in fear for her life from this drunken intruder who entered the apartment," thus verifying my story.

The case was summarily discharged and dismissed without prejudice by the same judge that had issued the warrant.

Months later, I return home after working patrol, thinking my past is finally behind me, when fate once more comes knocking.

I get to my apartment, and off to the corner of my eye I see three shapes in the shadows. "So what have we here?" I said. One of the shapes identifies himself and his companions as District Narcotics Cops. How unusual in my hallway! "Okay, so again guys, what's up?" They advise they have a stakeout based on information from a CI (confidential informant) that two subjects were going to burglarize a butcher shop down the street that actually was a front for a narcotics distribution center. The beef was that the drugs were in the beef and that was simply disgusting.

They said this was late arriving info and they hadn't time to set up a proper surveillance or plan and had just arrived themselves. They added they were shorthanded and could I assist them and if I had any heavy weapons at my apartment, that can be used. I reluctantly agreed, but my heart was certainly not in it. I went up to my apartment and retrieved a Browning 9mm Hi-Power (for me), a 30 cal. M-1 carbine (cherry, as in condition, not color) and an Ithaca 12 gauge shotgun. Their eyes widened when I brought the load down and someone asked, "Why do you have all this shit?" and I answered, "Bad neighborhood," "What's so bad about this neighborhood?" they asked. "Too much police action around here for my taste," was my cryptic answer. They assured me their CI information has been good so far and they were certain the thugs would come out the front and they'll handle it. All I have to do is get comfortable at the back and watch the fun. To the back of the store I go, and I settle down in the alley. I'm leaning against the porch thinking about dinner when I hear shouting and great commotion. Out of the back door 25 feet away, these guys come bursting out into the alley. It's now dark, very dark, and only one grimy 60 watt bulb is illuminating the area. All of a sudden dinner is not all that important and I am again focused. They stop a few feet after exiting the rear of the butcher shop and look right at me, silhouetted while they are still in shadow. I yell, "Police. Stop or I'll shoot," and the one asshole replies "You better shoot me fucker before I shoot you." This sounded like a very good idea so I let go one round from my 9mm and hit him square in the spleen. He goes down, and the other guy gives up with the other three mopes coming to my aid, a day late and a dollar short. For some reason all my current problems had to do with spleens, like I even know where one is.

We retrieve a side of beef and the drugs the cow was holding and a .22 Ruger automatic from the offenders. I think there may have been a porterhouse steak and some chops, but no one quite remembers what happened to them so I assume they got away. Not to worry. I doubt they got very far. The wounded guy is transported to the hospital and survived and I go along with the Vice Dicks to the station for the paperwork. The news has preceded me—Cohen does it again. It looked like a righteous shooting and when I get there the "Atta boys" are starting to flow. Just then the Dicks arrived as part of the shooting team, and it turns out I had history with both of the suspects and had arrested them previously. Routine questioning commenced, and then I was asked to hand over the 9mm Browning used in the shooting, which was standard operating procedure (SOP). I cleared the action and removed the rounds from the magazine and handed it over, along with the collected bullets. Several minutes later, both Dicks and the On-Watch Captain came into the interrogation room and they ask, "Is there something else you want to tell us?" and I answered, "Yes, there is." "Come clean, what do we not know that you feel is important?" "I haven't had my dinner yet, and I'm pretty darn hungry, also I gotta pee." They proceed to advise me that the gun I used was hot, and I say "What are you talking about?" and they say it was taken a couple months before in a burglary on the North West Side. "So where did you get the gun, officer?"

"Again, where did you get the gun?" I was asked. "Don't recall," I believe I answered. I was then told, "You are going to the West Side (where the county jail and courts are located) and you can tell it to the Grand Jury." "Do you have a bag?" "A bag?" "A trick bag," I responded. "What do you need a trick bag for?" "I am about to spill the beans and don't want anyone to slip on a stray." A trick bag described when a cop was really fucked up (You would be in the trick bag).

"Truth be told, I bought the gun from the partner of an officer who went through the Academy with me." "Who is that?" "Can't recall." "Grand Jury." "Oh yes, I bought the gun from Mike Calusi." "I was sitting down at Bert's having coffee when Mike asked before the three of us if I wanted to buy a 9mm for $100." "So who are the other guys at the table, and can they verify it." "There was Mike, of course, me, my partner Jack Marcus and Dennis Farina." They were subsequently brought into the investigation with Jack backing my story and, of course, Mike denying it, and Dennis backed his story. This was an utter and complete lie and copout, and frankly it surprised me. I had known Dennis from the Academy and though we were never partners I thought I had a good read on his character. I was wrong. This was a Mexican standoff and my career was on the line, so we were sent down to Reid (downtown) to take the lie box. The results of all four were inconclusive. So much for science. I was then sent to the Board, the final hearing on whether I would be retained or let go, or to reduce the charges. As luck would have it, one of the few straight arrows, a Captain, who was knowledgeable about my career, influenced the Board in my favor and I got away with a "30 day" suspension.

Needless to say, I was not very popular around the Department after this episode, depending on whose side you were on, and Dennis never spoke to me again after this happened. As a side note, Dennis later became an actor. Just recently, he was arrested at LAX for trying to carry a loaded gun on an airplane, and has since been hit with three charges based on that incident. This is still being worked as of this writing.

Looking back on my last three serious problems, the Ex IRS-spleen guy, the drug beef spleen shooting and the hot gun caper, I believe I did learn something of value. In retrospect, maybe I did hit "contestant number one" just a little harder than I had to, and I could have avoided that problem if I had been a little less enthusiastic. Had I not been an expert in the Martial Arts, my punch would not have been considered assault with a deadly weapon. Had I not offered to help the Narcotics Detectives,

I could have avoided the second incident. Had I not used my house gun, I would have avoided the entire hot gun situation, and on and on. Supposedly you learn from your mistakes and I had quite a good pile of learning material those days, but then no matter how careful you are the one thing that can always be counted on is that "shit happens."

A COMPLETE AND UTTER WASTE

Chapter 6

A few words about one of my least favorite subjects: gangs. Gangs have been part of the tapestry for all of recorded history and probably before that. Fine and good, a group of like-minded individuals is always in fashion: bird watchers, stamp collectors, concert goers and now"low life MF pissant leaches". Surrounding yourself with copies is always comfortable, but gangs from the 60s to this day denote rabble focused on antisocial activities. A baseball club is not a gang; it's a club. The Mob (first or second) is not a gang; it's an organization. A gang can be more than just a loose association, and starting in the 60s evolved from street thugs to organized dope pushers, extortionists and murderers. In my time, I have personally come to know several of the most infamous, whom I will discuss.

You notice I called them what I believe they are, but I also respect them as I would the scorpion or rattlesnake. Being dismissive or disrespectful of their potential is potentially a fatal mistake. In my view, there is nothing more dangerous or divisive in the country today than gangs. We fight wars in other countries against terrorists and fanatics. Yet some of the most violent, destructive and antisocial of all are Americans living here and disrupting our major cities.

The relevance of the gangs of the 60s through

the 80s is mirrored today in the world of Narco Terrorists who threatens all first world nations, including the United States, and who are as threatening as any others who belong to terrorist movements.

That is as it is and I have no solution, only observations. One misconception is that you have to be lacking in intelligence to belong to a gang or to rise in its hierarchy. The opposite is probably the case. Some of the most psychopathic gang members I have ever encountered are also among the most intelligent individuals I've known. One even had a photographic memory.

As an interesting exercise, go to an inner city school and speak to kids likely to gravitate to gang membership. Ask them questions about their country and they will have little idea what you are talking about. Show them photos of famous Americans or world leaders and the answer will be the same. Show them flash cards of weapons and they will identify each and every one and give you specs. This one is a Mac-10 with a silencer, cyclic rate of and in 9mm or 45 cal. That one is a Beretta 92FS, 9mm but comes in 10mm and 40 SW also. They will know these like earlier generations knew faces on baseball cards. These are not dumb people-misguided perhaps, but not lacking in native intelligence.

Their view of life is at odds with the rest of us. They view prison as higher education. Some of their relatives will always be incarcerated, and local heroes are those who died violently in gang warfare. Gangs are international today and there are thousands of them. Every major city is infested, and even the smallest towns and hamlets have theirs. Today gangs are armed as well as the police (sometimes better). They may view the taking of a life as nothing more than an initiation ritual and glorify killing in tattoos, rap and song. Colors are very important and wearing the wrong color at the wrong time in the wrong part of town can cost you your life in an instant. The most ruthless mob hit men hardly hold a candle to these guys, and gals. Whereas the mob tries hard not to hurt or kill civilians or police, gang members have no such limitations.

There are few old gang members, and this is almost a contradiction to the lifestyle. You live fast, flashy, colorfully and die young. There is a country western song, "Mothers, Don't Let Your Sons Grow up To Be Cowboys," but it seems more and more mothers in parts of every city see gang membership as a natural evolution for their kids. It is said you don't ever leave a gang—alive. Even the founders of some of the most notorious gangs in the country, through some happenstance living to middle age, are still subject to a quick and violent death at the hands of other gang members out to settle some old beef or to make a name, or a point or for no good reason at all.

I am only stating the obvious and to ignore this menace is to bury your head in the sand. In my view, this is Organized Crime today, but I saw it take flight in Chicago in the 60s as it did elsewhere in the country.

As a beat cop, I had to balance duty with common sense. Gangs are almost a force of nature, and while you should take reasonable precautions for that hurricane or cyclone, in a certain sense they will do what they will do no matter your preparations. First thing I always did was to know who was who in gangs and to keep my finger on the pulse of what was happening. I showed respect as one shows respect to a venomous snake, and I did not go out of my way to agitate, but I also made certain I was respected for the person I was. If they crossed me personally there would be a price to pay. All this really means is that if they were going to fuck with someone, it had better be in a District other than mine. And don't ever let me see you doing anything egregious because I will do my job on your face if you do. After this, it is pretty much live and let live.

Here's another thing to keep in mind. Ever hear that baby rattle snakes are as dangerous and deadly as the adults? They are. Gang members are becoming younger and younger, and their bullets kill you as fast as anyone else's. The youngsters are used for many violent activities since even in a killing they are typically subject only to juvenile penalties and can expect to leave kid prison (Gladiator School) by the time they are 25. This presents a particular problem to the beat officer when deciding whether or not to shoot. On one hand, you don't want to off a kid, but on the other hand, to hesitate can cost you or your partner your lives. No good answer here, only questions.

The one thing that separates gangs from other criminal enterprises is that a fundamental cornerstone of the outfit is that they give to their community. If someone is down on their luck, the local chapter will see that food or work goes to that individual. If someone is being leaned on, the local guys will sometimes help out. The idea is like that of Robin Hood. Look after the neighborhood where you live and they will look out for you. Gangs don't see it this way. Gangs, and this is an absolute statement, never do anything for anyone except themselves. They survive in their communities through abject fear and loathing and, as with any deadly viper, will strike anyone at any time who is in the crosshairs. Further, initiation frequently involves a violent crime or murder, often in the community. If gang members don't care if they live or die, why should they have any concern for others? They don't! I will now discuss particulars in my exposure to gangs during my career, but I will say for anyone interested that the enemy who most concerns me is not the enemy from without, but the enemy from within.

The principal gangs in Chicago in the 60s were the black gangs and a few notable white gangs. For the most part, the black gangs stayed in the ghettos except for the Cabrini Green Housing Project, which was located just west of the Magnificent

Mile, the Gold Coast. The Latino gangs were on the rise and would take on great influence in coming years. There were a few white gangs of significance such as the TJOs (Thorndale Jag Offs). They started off, as most gangs do, with street thugs and common criminals and evolved into a more disciplined organization. Some of their members were to become cops. Mostly, they did the usual vandalism, got high and terrorized the merchants. Until.... in the late 1960s the TJOs had two leaders of note, Joe Lanci and Gary Calley. Some people are destined for great things, and this goes for gang members also. In their case, their psychopathic tendencies, ruthlessness and sometimes keen intelligence would leave a mark and impact on the north side of Chicago. I had occasion to deal with these guys and a third member, Rufus Askew, during my beat days working our common turf. I had run-ins with several members, and with Rufus, during which I demonstrated and asserted myself in the way of a good beating. We had an unfriendly, but somewhat respectful détente, and in most cases, as these situations played out, we tried not to have our paths cross. They were always up to something, but it was understood nothing had better happen on my watch, or there would be a stiff price to pay. Occasionally I would meet with Calley on the street and he would brag about being beat up by a cop named Sam Serges Joseph, the single toughest, meanest, nastiest and most decorated cop in Chicago.

One afternoon, Lanci and Calley, while fucking

off and driving on the North side on Devon Avenue, saw a black man cleaning a window on a ladder and pulled out a shotgun and killed him. They were arrested in hours and subsequently were incarcerated in the State Penetentury at Joliet. Calley gets out on parole after several years and becomes a regular street thug and drug dealer and got involved in a shootout with the DEA (Drug Enforcement Administration) in the parking lot of Carsons Restaurant on the corner of Ridge and Ashland. He was returned to the Pen. Lanci's legacy is that he has become the enforcer for the Aryan Brotherhood while in the Pen and was moved from location to location where he caused mayhem and whatever. Some of the remaining members of the TJOs, having survived other encounters, died of overdoses. Still others graduated to regular family life and a career on the force.

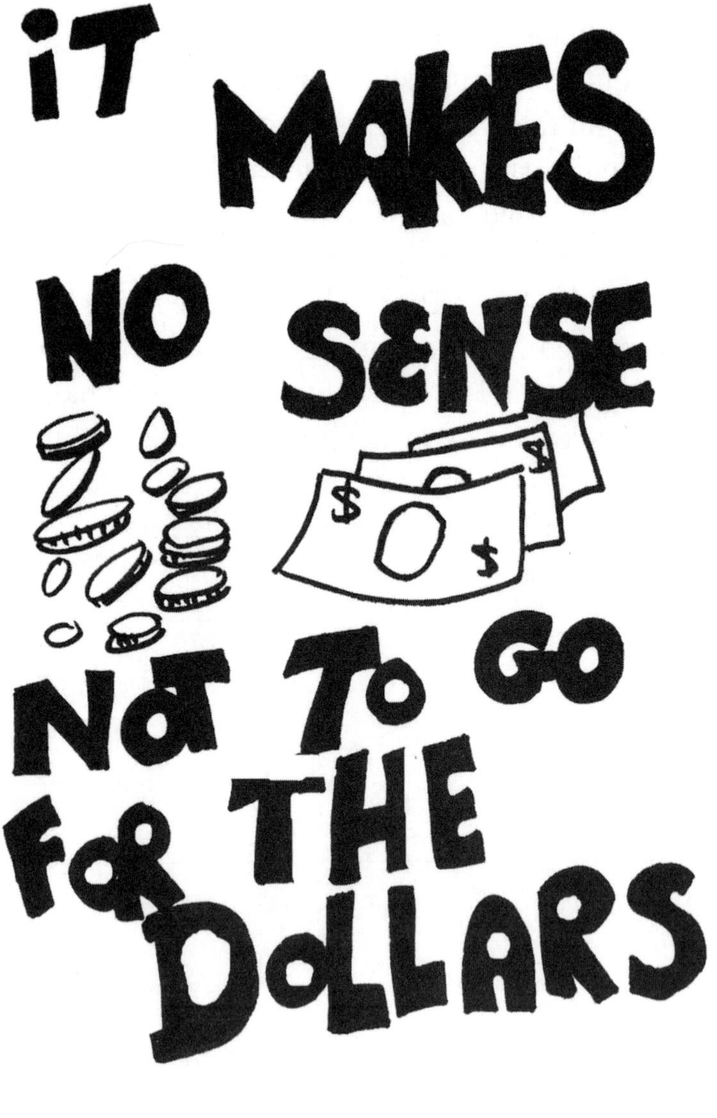
IT MAKES
NO SENSE
NOT TO GO
FOR THE
DOLLARS

Chapter 7

I am not out to justify or qualify my life or to offer up excuses for what I did while on the force, but I will say there were circumstances that came into play and that I and many of my compatriots were products of our time.

So what is it I am out to do by baring my soul and doing this book? For me, the answer is simple-to right history. Obviously, some stories have come out, but they speak to the gritty reality of individual cops and the hardships encountered. While I find these of interest, the bigger story of the pervasive corruption and dysfunction that was the disease has hardly been touched, and when mentioned at all, it is watered down to the point of a third-rate Hollywood B-movie script.

Considering that in 1966 there were perhaps 12,000 officers in the Chicago Police Department, and more than that in later years, this story has not been told. Let's say for sake of argument that the body total for police from 1966 to 1988 (the span of my career) was perhaps 30,000 officers—just not all at the same time. Now consider that this story, the story I am telling about the dishonesty and dysfunction of the Department and its members, has not been seriously recounted before (to my knowledge). That means that 30,000 individuals, including most of all the high ranking officers had direct or very good information that the corruption of the

Department happened. Yet no one has been willing to talk about it and gone mainstream. **That is a cover up of the most gigantic proportion**. As for myself... guilty as charged. I was not a good guy and don't view myself as a bad guy, I was simply an opportunist left alone in the candy store too long. I never sought out my own criminal activity, but did not look the other way when it came knocking. I have done some pretty egregious things in my life, but for me the one thing I am proud of is that I spent over 20 years in that corruption and yet was able to leave it behind and not be consumed by it. This is no mean trick; this is magic.

The time line is important for my story and it is a story in two parts. The "Old West" was for me and the force 1966–1980 and the "new way" was 1980 to 1988 and on. From current news reports, it appears things may have swung back the way of the Old West, but that's not for me to say. I would interject, however, there has to be a fundamental change in the dynamics of a situation for an earlier problem not to resurface, and I have seen no such effort regarding the Chicago PD. In the "good old days" there was little due process, no Miranda Rights or Escobedo Ruling and little if any forensics. Back then it was the mean streets, shoot or be shot, stand your ground or get out of town. That was the day of the freelancer, the cowboy and the peace officer with a six-gun (though peace had little to do with it). So you might ask why otherwise well intentioned young men became cops and I would first say only a few were well-intentioned. Most grew up in the area and knew the career they were embarking on. That career paid $90 a week in 1966 dollars. If I were being forthright in my dissertation, I would have to admit that while I was making $90 per week, taxable, as a rookie cop, I was also clearing around $300 a week, tax free, as an opportunist…. I would also point out that I didn't try all that hard and those around me were doing much better and approached it more as a business. I would say most everyone (but not all) were on the take to some degree, but again I can speak only of those I knew. Since I traveled from District to District throughout my time as a cop and found this pervasive everywhere I went, I have to conjecture that it was pretty much universal. I worked with many who viewed being a cop as a means to an end and an inconvenience to be tolerated while the real rewards were reaped. Would these same guys pull a complete stranger from a burning car or engage in a shootout if happening upon a robbery? Yes, they would. That is the absurd nature of this screwy world we inhabited. What made matters worse is that management, mid-level on up (lieutenants and up) were fully engaged in the deception so it was the inmates running the asylum.

To add to the mix, there was outdated technology, such as radios that used tubes, that needed to be heated to work. This meant the car must be on for the radio to work and, if a cop were to go into a building, he was away from communications entirely. There was also no air conditioning or power steering. You were essentially attached by a cord to a 2500 pound radio that didn't move.

The few good people who entered the force quickly opted out as soon as they came to their senses or they hide as a "Desk jockey." What was left were the lifers such as myself; and even I eventually came to the realization that this was no way to live. This brings me back to my beginning statement and I believe it applies to me and most that I worked with: we were obviously not all good and not all bad, but we spent time being very bad and very good, so we were fractured and hardened and we coped as best we could. Nobody said you had to stay a cop; that was your decision. Nobody held a gun to your head and said you can't leave as is purported to be done by the Mob; at its essence being a Chicago cop was just a job, but it had a way to satisfy as few other jobs could.

When night fell and I went on duty (My favorite time), it was magic hour. Where else can you wear what you want (If in civies or plain clothes), be allowed (not required) to carry a gun or two, given a hot car, lights and siren and permitted the run of the city come hell or high water. If I were undercover, which I often was, it was dress up and game time and the city and its environs were my playground. If I was having a bad day I could beat the crap out of some deserving lowlife and go home content, another day's fine work accomplished.

During my early years, I was single and enjoying the fruits of my labor. Let's say I had little occasion to meet the librarian and more than ample opportunity to get to know the hooker, party girl and opportunist. A different breed of cat prowls the street after dark and it is intoxicating. I dressed well, drove some fine rides, ate at great places, was feared and admired, and the world was pretty much mine for the taking. I have to admit I was hardened in those days and did not choose to see the softer side of things. In my world, everyone was damaged goods, including me, and nobody need apologize for that. It was live hard and die young—and who gave a shit anyway?

Let me say, life and death on the streets was never like the movies, never. If you shot someone they shit in their pants, vomited all over the place or had their brains plastered over the person next to them. Death is ugly and always disfiguring. If you were the most drop-dead beautiful woman in the world and had died the day before yesterday, nature would turn you into a maggot-infested amusement park and all the rides would be open. The smell is like nothing you ever encountered before and seemed to stick to you forever. A dead person is no different than a 150 pound roast left in the back yard for a couple days in the hot sun and humidity, a pretty unpleasant thing. Hardly a day went by that I didn't encounter at least one dead person, and the revulsion never grew old. It's sad, but you tend to look at the living differently when you become so calloused and accustomed to death; you also treat people differently. It wasn't until I married and had children that I started to soften and see another side. In those early days I was hard, uncaring and calloused, a bully and a force to be reckoned with. It's no statistical accident that the majority of people who married when the man enters the Academy do not remained married long. There is something that cannot be shared or communicated about this job, something forbidden, something shameful and something of a guilty pleasure that comes with the badge. And it is a narcotic, have no doubt about that.

Something feeds and nurtures the primitive part of the beast that comes from hunting, searching, pursuing, engaging and controlling or killing the quarry. There is always the promise of something deadly and raw around every corner, the hunter and the hunted, the good guy and the bad guy, those who will live and those who will die, the kill; that is just so basic. It repels and at the same time attracts and once tasted is almost impossible to ignore. You are in a fraternity with like-minded individuals, a gang, a mob if you will. You share secrets, vows, confidences, you cover each other's backs and rely on each other at the worst of times and then recall them with vivid retention at a bar hours later. There are somedays when you experience the worst there is and others when you honestly feel they should charge admission to be able to play this great game. Understand my use of the word "Game" was no mistake; this life becomes the ultimate Cops and Robbers game in which reality has a sharp cutting

edge and consequences are real, but so are the pleasures. Nothing compares to the pleasures. Ask an
old man who was in combat during WWII and he
will say that it was terrible, that it was mind-numb-
ing frightening and by far the best part of his life.
Just how it is. All else pales by comparison.

As I said, it isn't as depicted in the movies and
TV. To say it's never black and white is a gross
understatement, and the best I can offer is that it is
many shades of gray, or in this case blue.

Maybe in the end it's all a balance (was more
good done than evil?). In my case at least, I believe that to be true. I changed lives, ended lives
and had my life changed as a consequence. There
was never a master plan, no good intent, no evil intent, it was merely day-to-day survival. As an il-
lustration, some drivers look one car length ahead,
some look ten car lengths and some a mile ahead, I
never looked beyond the ornament on the front of
my hood, (When there were such things), and it was
only later in life that I started to look farther down
the road and plan.

To this day I don't feel bad about my early
years as a cop and if anything view it as some sort
of a grand adventure. I knowingly entered that life
and very deliberately left it 20 years later. As I said
at the start of this chapter, I feel no need to do pen-
ance or offer up excuses for those things I did that
were beyond the pale and have no desire to live on
the accolades of those things I did that were very
right and acknowledged. What I see when I look at

my time on the force is a blend of all things before I set my life into more defined and civilized pursuits. I write this book therefore not to offer contrition but rather to simply set the record straight. I can speak firsthand about those years and report with some detachment what happened behind closed doors and out of the sight of others. I am crusading for nothing other than to right the lies of past expediency and to set part of the record straight.

Chapter 8

My reputation usually did my talking for me, but then there were those times when something more physical or creative was called for.

When I had a beef with another cop we would just drop our gloves and whale on each other. I never lost these fights because I rarely entered a fight I didn't know I could win. I made a very conscious effort to network and this pulled my nuts out of the ringer on many occasions.

You never get away scot-free, of course; there is always the piper to pay. As I have learned, good intentions are never rewarded, and I was not all that familiar with good intentions. I was on patrol and stopped a motorist for something. This fellow hands me his wallet with a folded $20 bill and a gave me a shit load of attitude. I told him to keep his fucking money, that he was getting the ticket. He was so pissed that he went directly to the station and complained to my watch commander Francis (Frannie) O'Conner (I think he was Polish or something) and, when I got back to the station, it was into his office for a chat. He says, "Lad, what are you trying to do, mess things up for us other working stiffs?" and I answered truthfully, "I just didn't like that fucker's face and didn't want his twenty." Francis told me in deadly earnest, "There are three things a police officer doesn't do: 1) he doesn't get cold 2) he doesn't get wet and 3) he doesn't get hungry." "You had better get with the program and while you are at it lose the cookie duster over your lip, you look like some Nigger Cop on the South Side." He had such a way with words, but then so did I. "Fuck you and the horse you rode in on," I intoned, or words to that effect.

Next day, I found myself on a one-man foot patrol at 63rd and Cottage Grove, which was just down the street from the Muslim Temple of Eliza Mohammad. Almost immediately, cars started to slow down as they drove by. Some honked, and a crowd started to gather. I was the only white piece on a chessboard full of black pieces, and things didn't look too good. A few toughs came on over and started to rag on me and the crowd grew. I figured I was dead anyway, so when someone reached for my gun, I drew it and pistol-whipped the fucker across the face and then smashed the guy next to him. I grabbed the one that looked like the ringleader and pulled him right up to me. I shoved my .357 right into his loose pants and smashed the barrel into his nuts. Making a show of cocking my piece, I said, "Being a big black stud, you must have really big balls but if anyone gives me any trouble, I will turn you into a her." And just to make my point, I raked the gun back a couple of inches and cut him most unpleasantly with the ramped front sight. You could have heard a pin drop, and my new closest friend was starting to turn white. Someone in a shop close by called the District Station and almost instantly several patrol cars showed up to disperse the crowd. Frannie never mentioned this again and I kept my cookie duster. Shit, you just don't mess with a man's upper lip, you just don't.

The pay was $90 a week as I mentioned, but that wasn't all that bad, even without the side income. Meals were usually free, cleaning was half price, flowers free, booze free, entertainment free, and the list goes on. Most eating establishments liked the cops to eat there since it ensured no robberies or other problems (Such as citations for triple parking out front).

One day my partner and I were working the wagon (Paddy, not welcome) and thought a Chicago deep dish pizza would be just what the doctor ordered. The Department was lax to blind on most things, but a hard line was drawn governing the time you get for lunch; you get only 30 minutes for lunch and "Downtime." The way you work around this is to not call in "Up" from the previous call (pretending to do paperwork) and to drop by the restaurant (in this case the pizza parlor) and place the order. This is what we did. We parked and went in and placed our order with the waitress, and then we left, planning to return in around 20 minutes. Off we go, back we come, and again we sit down. Nothing, nothing at all, and we are the only customers in the joint. Finally, we get up and talk to the waitress, who advises us she never put in our order; said she thought we were still making up our minds on what we wanted. I was so steaming pissed, I said none too politely, "You know how little time we have for lunch and you deliberately fuck us over." The next thing is the manager, this pimply little toad, waddles over and is belligerent and showing absolutely no respect. "So what you gunna do about it?" he says. Wally, my partner wanted to deposit the fucker into the salad bar but being that I had now matured, I had a better idea. With this we took our leave. I guess they were abused by some other cops who pushed the free thing too far, but the conversation never quite got around to that. Wally and I are students of unconventional warfare and knew exactly what to do. We drove the wagon over to skid row and picked up around a dozen of the filthiest, most disgusting winos we could find and piled them into the wagon. We drove back to the shop and told all our passengers that the manager of the pizza place wanted to do something special for his "neighbors" and was giving out free pizza. All they had to do was to go in, sit down and not leave until each got his own super large deluxe deep dish pizza. It got even better: this offer was good for an entire week so they needed to come back each day for their meal. Well, our pizza manager was none too pleased and actually called the station to complain. Having briefed the station beforehand, pointing out that this was for the good of the Department, they ignored him. A week later, the owner fired the manager and waitress and life was once more back to normal. Point made. Don't mess with the man with a plan and never, ever stand between a cop and his pizza.

EVERY SUPER HERO NEEDS A SIDEKICK

Chapter 9

Now settle down, I am not suggesting I am a superhero—hardly. There are those days when your cape just needs to go to the cleaners and then you become just a street cop or whatever.

Enough of this. Now for what I really want to talk about. In life and in nature there are those instances when a symbiotic relationship develops and when that happens it's a thing of beauty. Nobody can do it alone, nobody can cover all the bases and not leave something open that may be harmful. Butch had Sundance, Batman had Robin, the Lone Ranger had Tonto and I had an Irish kid named Brian McNamara. You can also say Brian had me as a sidekick also.

I was working the East Chicago District in 1969-1970. This area was divided into two distinct parts or sectors; East was the Gold Coast Michigan Avenue and Rush Street where Frank Sinatra hung out at Jilly's Bar or Mr. Kelly's, which had live entertainment from around the country. On Wacker Drive, the London House nightly had every notable Jazz musician sitting down to spread the magic. The West part of the District, where I worked, contained the Cabrini Green Housing Project, which is most closely and accurately compared to Beirut or Baghdad. These were tall, ugly high-rises controlled by the gangs and was no-man's land as far as the cops or any sane person were concerned. Division Street, a main east-west artery going from the Lake all the way west, was routinely closed after dark due to sniper fire from the projects. I was assigned to patrol this area along with my best friend, my Ithaca 12 ga. Police shotgun. I found that nothing says "Excuse me, sir" like the ratcheting sound of charging a 12 gauge. Chunk, chunk, and you have everyone's attention. I was not partnered with Brian, but we worked adjoining beats in-one man cars and, if a hot call came in that I could be in trouble, Brian would show up and also the other way around. We simply looked after one another.

Brian was quite a guy (still is); he is believed to have belonged to a motorcycle gang prior to his entering the force, looked like a Hollywood leading man, but was scarred from head to toe from knife fights and other altercations. This only accentuated his good appearance, and he wore his scars well as badges of courage. Brian could go into any bar or night spot in the 18th District and would not be allowed to pick up the tab, ever. No one would ever charge him, he was that special. He stood 6'4" with 5% body fat and had a presence about him that could not be ignored.

If I responded to a call that advised "shots had been fired," I could expect to see Brian show up to, as he put it, "cover my Jew ass," and I would respond by saying, "I am always there to cover your Turkey ass, you MF." He had one funny aspect to his character though. He loved (and I mean really loved) animals. At our Station garage we had abandoned animal cages all about and he made sure stray dogs, cats, rabbits and most anything else with four legs were kept there rather than transported. He would check them every day, feed them and look to their welfare. To be transported meant almost instant death to the animals, but he found homes for most in his care. It was hard to say no to this man and he saved dozens of wonderful animals.

He and I had and kept horses. One day he calls me up and says, "Let's transport our horses from their stables to the Lakefront and go riding on the jogging path." Chicago didn't have a Mounted Unit at that time so we were it. He shows up with a horse trailer and is clothed in a Cavalary riding outfit with long black boots and a 7th Cavalary hat. You could almost hear "Boots and Saddles" playing in the background. We get to the jogging path and are unloading our animals when we see a fair amount of blood on the floor of the trailer. It seems my horse cut himself on a rusty nail just above his hoof and it was almost three inches long and deep. He said, "You can't ride him like that," and I answered "No, we need to get that fixed." He has me get into the cab after we reload the animals and I say, "Shit, the nearest large animal vet is an hour away." He answers, "Don't worry about it." Off we go and a few minutes later we pull in to Emergency at Columbus Hospital. He runs in and comes back with a full complement of Emergency personnel. "Where is the patient?" they ask. "Here," he answers, and points to my horse. One of the medical personnel said " I'm sorry we can't help you, thats a horse and we only give medical treatment to humans." Brian went up to the fuck (medical personnel guy) and whispered something in his ear. I'm not sure what he said exactly, but I think it had something to do with on how long the guy planned on living. Minutes later, my mount was stitched up and ready to go; Brain had that kind of sway over people.

One day, I answer a radio call from him and he says through great pain, "Hey buddy, need your help here," and he gives me an address. I arrive at the scene and there he is, swinging in a circle, clockwise, with a giant German Shepherd's teeth clamped to his crotch. He is spinning, the dog is off the ground and they are doing this nice spinning dance move, only he is screaming. "Get the fucking dog off me, now!" I say, "Want me to shoot it?" and he answers, "Only if you want me to shoot you." I pried the dog off and Brian spent two months on medical. His voice was noticeably higher after that.

Sometimes it's noteworthy just to have such a good friend and to be such a good friend to someone. I have to smile when I talk about Brian and the good times we had together. Nothing dramatic, just good times with a good person.

TO SERVE AND COLLECT

POLICE

Chapter 10

It's always a good idea to know who you are doing business with and, without question, police and crooks share a professional bond.

In all things you have a range of personalities and traits that can be assigned to a individual. With cops you have the few straight arrows, the bent arrows and the broken arrows, but along with this you have the professional, the opportunists, the sadists and the unbalanced. Crooks also fall in much the same categories. You have on one extreme the professional crook, either syndicated with an organization or working freelance as an individual; you have the opportunist, the sadists and the unbalanced.

I once asked why a person should keep a light on in the backyard and on the front stoop: I answered, " The light lets the part-time crook know that he should leave your place alone and hit your neighbor, while the professional burglar or the burglar on dope will not be dissuaded.

One of the hardest crimes to solve and the most difficult perpetrator to apprehend is the professional burglar, the second story man. Unless you actually get them leaving a building (or obviously still inside, you have little to charge the individual with. These people are the specialists, the pros. They rarely if ever carry weapons, will not put up a fight and will be as cooperative as anyone when cornered. They are the white collar criminals working in a blue collar environment.

I always considered myself a professional and had no problem sitting down for coffee and chat with a professional on the other side. This was in no way a cooperative undertaking, but it was a good forum for discussing trends, players and dynamics.

Respect is pivotal for working with anyone. Lack of respect or perceived disrespect, then as now, is the quickest way to conflict. I gave respect where respect was due, both to other members of the force and to those on the other side. Some fellow cops deserved respect and many others deserved nothing at all. It may have just been me, but I rarely if ever respected anyone in a position of authority. The reason for this is that few people of rank got there deservedly and most made it through cronyism and favor.

With criminals, if they treated me well, I was, particularly later in my career, more likely to treat them well, but I had a hair trigger and did not take fools lightly. Any attitude or challenge was met with overwhelmingly brutal force. Most on the streets knew this, so I only occasionally had to employ violence. I did not limit this rule of the road to the criminal and would just as quickly deck a fellow officer if the situation merited it. I wonder if this had anything to do with my overall lack of progress through the ranks over the years.

I tried not to burn too many bridges since I was a fairly permanent figure in the streets and the thug I arrest today may be the one I will need too deal with next week or next year. Further, when gangs are involved, it is necessary to find a workable balance for all to exist. Gangs are territorial, violent, established and vindictive, and it simply cannot be all out warfare all the time; the body count would be unacceptable. A type of understanding or truce is usually reached, an accommodation in which certain activities and territories are generally permitted, but excesses or anything blatantly outside the norm will be dealt with harshly by the authorities. Even the Allies directly after WW2 had to hire Nazi officers to run the utilities and other functions in the then defeated Germany. High members of NATO today served in the German army and air force during the war, but then circumstance makes for strange bedfellows.

The important thing as a beat cop or Tactical Officer is to be known and to have your reputation precede you. In this line of work, as in no other, surprises, (Other than birthday parties) are typically bad and to be avoided.

In theatrical productions there is a style called "Theater of the Absurd," and in a way that phrase summed up my 20 years in the Chicago Police Department. The first few weeks were the Academy, and halfway through my father died unexpectedly. He was a Precinct Captain, which is a well respected mid-level political appointment that carries with it good weight and influence.

My mother and father did not want me to enter the Department, but I was stubbornly determined after talking to a Police Sergeant who lived three blocks down. While other men my age were being drafted or simply joined the service for Vietnam, I decided to fight my good fight at home. My draft board gave me an occupational deferment knowing of my plans to join the Police Force.

The Academy lasted 14 weeks and was right next to a hot dog stand. We kept our windows open all the time, so I learned to be a cop at the same time I learned to lust after hot dogs and Polish sausage.

My first warning to the rampant corruption in the CPD (Chicago Polcie Department) should have been the insistence the instructors placed on this vague "something" that we would each have to experience and decide for ourselves, but they wouldn't come out and just say what that something was. Obviously they were talking about being on the take and that this was both institutionalized and both accepted and widely practiced.

I should have sensed a warning when upon reporting to my first assignment at the 20th District was in essence told to forget all I have just been taught at the Academy.

Somewhere along the line, I had stepped through the looking glass and was now in this institutionalized insanity that was more organized crime than police work. You had to ask yourself who were the good guys and who were the bad guys; instead of black and white, all I ever saw were shades of gray.

Last on the list was City Government itself and

our Boss, the Honorable Richard J. Daley, Mayor of Chicago and master of our universe. The Police Force constituted his private army and nothing happened in the windy city without his express permission. Government in Chicago was more a monarchy than a representational form of government.

I was the proverbial kid in the candy store: fast ride, fast women, really cool action, one of a kind friends, adventure all the time and a steady stream of rewards to help finance the lifestyle—something right out of a movie. Cops and robbers, good vs. evil, fastest draw, best shot and as with all 20-year-olds, the invincibility that only comes with lack of experience.

I carried the biggest, baddest gun, was tall, well built and someone to be feared. My playground was typically at night, and Gotham had nothing on Chicago after the sun went down. I put it on the line, cheated death on many occasions and had a reputation that would always precede me. My reputation spoke volumes and allowed me to part the waters without really trying. I was a hero in my own mind, a favorite of reporters, papers and TV, and pretty soon started to believe the hero status assigned me. When the sun set, I would strap on my gun and it was almost as if I were affixing my cape to my shoulders. I felt I was saving my city and that I was immune to the slings and arrows, but that's youth speaking. Such a grand adventure, I almost wanted to pay the city for the fun I was having. Back then, the filth had yet to wear through my defenses and it was at first, for lack of a better term, a magnificent adventure.

Time, physical damage, mental images that would not go away, the filth that would not wash off finally started to take their toll as is commonplace with all officers on the street, This was followed by discrimination. (an age old practice) of killing the spirit and belittling the individual by upper management also took its pound of flesh.

I experienced the highs, lows and the ridiculous from the inside out, a Fellini movie that was always just a bit out of sync, a sound track that didn't precisely go with the moving lips, the grating of approaching mental strain.

I was this way until my marriage years later and credit my wife and children with saving my life and giving me the gift of normality.

What isn't appreciated about action-real physical, deadly action—is that it is almost a narcotic. What satisfies today is left wanting a week later. So you seek the next better experience. And you cheat death just a little closer to the line. Intellectually, you know that if you walk around the lip of an active volcano long enough, fate will have you step in the wrong place and that with the breaking of the rim you teeter between life and a fiery death.

If you keep seeing the bet and then raising it, eventually you will need to put your cards down on the table and see if the adrenalin rush you always sought was anything more than a self-indulgence. It was not that I had a death wish, but I never wore tired of pushing the envelope and seeking the new and the more bizarre, to see where that invisible barrier is that would kill me or let me prevail.

If a sane person were to look at my early life, the only conclusion they would come away with is that I was a day patient on leave from the "Theater of the Absurd."

People become cops for all sorts of reasons. There are the altruistic reasons such as patriotism, family history, television and such, and then there is the reason many joined the Chicago Police Department—and that is to make money. The pay was and is poor so I am not suggesting honest motives, but rather the common knowledge that to be on the force and on the street meant to be on the take. Said more politely, the term would be alternative revenue sources.

As will be detailed in later chapters, the Police Department was essentially a multi-tier revenue producing machine. Traffic cops would routinely take money to let an offender go, and in fact, those who frequented night spots in the city typically had a 20 dollar bill tucked just behind their driver's license. There were rules, even for criminal behavior. An example would be that you never try to shake down a driver in front of his wife and kids, leave anyone smoking a pipe alone and don't take a guy's last dollar. If you abused the established rules, you potentially brought ruin down on others, perhaps killing the golden goose. So it was not beyond the realm of possibility that to save the goose it might be the offender who paid the ultimate price. Serious business carries with it the potential of serious consequences. For bread and butter extra income, traffic was considered the prize to be lusted after, and you found that once it was achieved, traffic cops rarely accepted a promotion that would take them away from the easy pickings.

From there things became a bit more sophisticated. You wanted to be the first to a suicide so you had a chance to ransack the place before others arrived. Picking up drunks in the paddy wagon also presented a host of opportunities. If it were a slow night, the driver of the wagon and his assistant might simply roll drunks and leave them where they dropped.

Up the ladder, some cops would burglarize a place and then report the crime. The funny thing is that the merchandise taken was often in the trunk of the patrol car calling in the burglary.

Of course there were protection schemes and influence rackets, but these were usually left to the first Chicago Mob, with a payoff for the street cop to just look the other way. The big payday would come from raids on drug or cat houses. If there was a scuffle or a gun fight with runners, most of the units would take off after the bad guys while you were left to "secure" the scene, which meant five or ten minutes to scout the place for cash or drugs and secure them in a bag or case that you had with you for just such an occasion.

I had my ethics and my rules, and rule number

one was that I would never risk going to jail for a minor offense. No petty crimes for me, thank you.

One day I was breaking in a new kid just out of the Academy and we were driving night patrol (My favorite). After a while, with the kid driving, he says he wants to make some traffic stops. "Why?" I asked him. "I need the cash," comes the answer. "You need the cash, do you?" "Yeh." "You really need some cash?" "That's what I just said, isn't it?" "Okay kid, pull up over there, by the Liquor Store." He pulls up and stops and I get out and come around to the driver's side window and pull my revolver out of its holster. "What the hell are you doing?" he yells. "We're going to rob the fucking liquor Store," I answer. "WHAT?" he screams. "I told you kid, I won't go to jail for a petty crime, so if you really need cash that bad lets knock over this place." He backed out and we resumed patrol. Point made.

What would I have done had he gone along with my plan? Well, I don't honestly know.

Chapter 11

I realize one thing I have not done well so far in this book is in giving you, the reader, a yardstick on which to measure the money involved in the business of Chicago's Other Mob. In point of fact, I can't even guess this number myself and, as it turns out, nor could the Federal Government and others in their various investigations. Still, I can give you some idea of how it worked (Or works) and you can surmise what is involved. But, as a previous Secretary of Defense once said, "Billions here and Billions there and pretty soon we are talking about real money."

I would start once again with me as a part-time opportunist and then contrast this to what I would say are serious players. A comparison here might help. When you go to the supermarket, your wife might say, "Dear, while you are at the store, please buy some potatoes." You may reasonably inquire, "What type and size?" "You know, the white ones." "Do you want the little round ones you serve with peas and a cream sauce, the mid-size you mash or the really big ones you bake?" "I want the really big potatoes dear." Okay, so now you have a range. I was a very little potato, the type you serve with cream sauce and peas. The serious player would be the mashing type and the made guys or the guys with a plan. The ones with position and opportunity would be the really big baking potatoes.

That said, let's put some general dollars with the potatoes. I said before that in a typical month I might see $300 in 1966 dollars (Tax free, of course), and I was as part-time and a casual participant as there probably was. A patrolman who was serious about this would approach it as a business. Some even set goals per night, week and month by which to gauge their efforts. As a guess I would say such people, on their own, would see maybe $2000 per month. From here you go the mashing type potatoes, which would be players who were part of a scheme or mini-organization or who had something worthwhile to sell (i.e., testimony in trials as bought by defense lawyers or looking the other way when the mob was doing business). Those might see $2000-$3500 per month. It's hard to quantify the big potatoes since their revenue came from many things.

An informant was heard to say that he paid the Chief of Detectives (Now serving time in federal prison) $1,000–2,000 per month and a new car every two years.

I may be off in these numbers some, but I wanted to provide a range so you can appreciate this is not a casual business such as free baseball tickets and a nice dinner now and then; this is very serious business with very serious consequences. No office pool, this is big time, organized effort that has been institutionalized, standardized and normalized.

That said, I would now like to talk now about

how this worked at its various levels. At the lower to mid-levels, again for the real players there were two parts to the program. First, you needed to make the money, and second you needed to flow some of the proceeds to others as a tribute for their participation in the organization. If a patrolman were eventually promoted and now stayed full-time at the station, perhaps as a Desk Sergeant, Scheduler or other duty, they no longer had the opportunity to go out and make their own bucks, but were still valuable to those on the streets as far as work schedules, partnering, patrol areas, assignments and oversight. A percentage of the take rightfully went to these individuals; it was their due.

Everyone had opportunities to make money, and this ran the gamut from lucrative business of traffic cops who stop motorists at night and are paid not to enforce a ticket to the street cop who is bought off by the defense attorney to change a story or throw the case to the detective (The detective is paid by the Mob to not pursue particular individuals). There is always money to be made in being sure a beat officer is looking the other way during protection payoffs or drug deals and of course, for vice to leave certain individuals and locations alone or at least advise of coming raids. Going up the ladder, things become more sophisticated between lawyers and judges and senior police officials, but this is pretty invisible. Of note is that senior police officials (very senior), lawyers on both sides and judges have been charged, tried, convicted and sent to prison on precisely these charges. It would be naive to think politicians are not involved in such goings-on and, in fact, a previous Governor of Illinois, the man who chaired the commission to investigate the Chicago Police Department was himself subsequently convicted on receiving payoffs and went to prison. It is known that officers of lower rank in the Department enjoyed more income in some months than the very heads of the Department. It is also known that Made Members of the First Chicago Mob were also police officials who did both their police work and bag work for the Mob.

I am not saying there were no straight arrows (honest cops) on the force then or now. It's just that I met so very few of them. It's hard to swim upstream when everyone else is headed downstream.

I want to make another point clearly so there is no question or ambiguity over where I stand on some issues. I don't care what their extracurricular activities were, if an officer died on the job doing his police responsibility, I feel the slate is wiped clear and this person is a hero for all time. It would be his job to pull a burning person out of a fire or to engage in a gun battle if unavoidable. These guys were cops first, thugs or thieves later, and I will not ever despoil their good names or withhold the respect that is due them.

Their families, the department, the city, the state and the nation all have reason to be proud of what it takes for a man to risk all for someone he doesn't know, and I would never take that away from the individual or their families. No person is ever one-dimensional. Things get complicated, but I respect that it's somewhere between very difficult and almost impossible to break from the status quo. Most people simply do not have the ability or strength in them.

In retrospect, it is harder to explain and qualify, but at the time taking advantage of one's position seemed normal and common place. A distinction can be drawn between passive excess, as I would refer to it, and active thievery. This may be a moot point, but as one who participated, I see some difference in sharing a payoff or accepting a gratuity or relieving a dead person of some cash and those who would actively rob establishments, strong-arm for pay or engage in drug activity. This may be splitting hairs, but to me the degree of malfeasance needs to enter the equation somewhere. Please, once again, this is not meant to qualify or seek atonement for my transgressions, but is put forward in an attempt to allow the reader insight into those times, those crimes and those who were involved. To go beyond explanation would be gratuitous and self-serving. Let's just say that when I or others I knew were on the wrong side of the equation, we believed there were degrees of behavior and consequence that related directly to the dishonest activity engaged in (i.e, some things were simply much worse than others).

At this point, you may be of a mind that I was quite a player, but in fact, I was at best a part-time participant. My official police folder, quite thick with disciplinary issues and commodations, never once mentions anything having to do with money or property issues. I would like to think I was close enough to have a very good idea what was happening, what was what, who was who, and yet not be a card carrying member of the club. It's not that at time I didn't want to be in the club, more that as a Jew, I would not be welcome. In 20 years, I feel I have cut sectionally through most of the Department. I have seen most of what can be seen and have as good a lay of the land as any one. Yet I was far enough removed from the day-to-day extravagances of this behavior to be able to relate it accurately and not make excuses.

The mistake is to treat these as petty abuses or crimes. This vast scale of participation demands organization, wide scale cooperation at all levels, and-most of all-serious amounts of generally untraceable cash. To many, becoming a police officer was merely the initiation into the club or institution. This should not be confused with "Organized crime" or the First Mob, which goes by several names; though made members (permanent members who have achieved tenure and passed certification) may also be members of the force as police officers (Chicago's other or second Mob), not many members of the police were also members of the First Mob. Confusing, because even if you were not a made member of the First Mob, you could still be an associate member or "Associate" of the First

Mob and belong to the police. This is quite convoluted. In a sense, this it was like the Roosters (police) having the Foxes (Made members of the Mob) help work to guard the hen house. Bad idea, but that's just how it was.

Finally, there are the politicians and their involvement; but this is hazy for me. It defies all logic to accept that politicians lacked significant insight into or participation in these illegal activities. You reach the inescapable conclusion that either they must have been involved up to their eyeballs: Or they are guilty of the greatest malfeasance in office of any official for all of time. For them to want us to think they didn't know of what was happening right under their noses; this is just too far a stretch for most, but it is what we are supposed to believe.

NEIGHBORHOOD POLICING

Chapter 12

When working the good guy, police side of my career (which was most of the time), I and those around me tried to be good cops. The trouble comes in defining what a good cop is and isn't. I never, ever played by the rules and I was really bad with authority. I knew my career was going nowhere since higher rank always, always, required connections. These connections could be with the church, the machine, with fraternal organizations or criminal enterprise (The Mob), but a lone Jew in this stew stood no chance. For me, that was actually fine as I never could view myself riding a desk and eating donuts.

Some very decorated cops were promised promotion but never saw that materialize. Each time a new Captain would come on board the promises were repeated: "Just give it a little time and the job will be yours," and it never came to be. Whether this was due to the Good Old Boys Club or some other conspiracy, if you were effective on the street, that's where they were likely to keep you. This hardens a man and kills the soul, and in one case a cop (Sam) I knew, just turned to the dark side, causing the city's felons to pay the terrible price. He was the product of the system, a victim of the system.

He was one of the most decorated officers ever on the force and a favorite of the press but was kept spinning his wheels. Whether he took too many hits, perhaps his bravery put him in harm's way once too often, maybe it was his chemistry, but he was unique, completely an army by himself. He was invited to an interview show as being the most highly decorated cop in Chicago at that time, along with his counterpart from the N.Y.P.D. At the interview the New York cop, a Captain, was introduced and was astounded to learn our guy was still a patrolman. This set the embitterment and summed up how he was viewed by his Department. He was okay on the streets where he could be his effective self, but he didn't have the respect, the connections or the confidence of upper management to be entrusted with rank. Because of this, he felt he was strictly being viewed as a beast of burden and on top of that no respect as well.

Sam was very influential in my development as a street cop. He was feared by everyone and it made little if any difference if you were a cop or crook if you were standing in his way. I was reporting to the squad late one evening and went in the back door. There were suspects cuffed to the wall almost like in a medieval dungeon, and as I walked up the hall, I saw Sam interrogating one suspect in a side room. The guy was sitting in a chair and Sam was screaming at him and then he took his nickle plated .45 automatic from his shoulder holster and shoved it into the puke's mouth. The thug's eyes grew to the size of saucers and Sam raked the gun back hard, cutting the roof of his mouth open with the front sight and sending teeth flying across the room. I just kept on walking; none of my business. I heard later the new Watch Commander, a recently promoted Captain, also walked by and saw something similar to what I witnessed, but he made the mistake of thinking he could or should do something about it. He barged in and went up to Sam and demanded to know what the hell he thought he was doing. Sam spun around, slammed the Captain into the wall. He stuck the bloodied .45 in his face and said in a ice-cold monotone, "If you ever question me or my methods again, I will kill you, I will kill your wife, your mother, your mother-in-law, your kids, your dog, and if you have one, your fuckin' parakeet." He then turned around and continued with the interrogation. The Captain scrambled out of the room and nothing more was ever mentioned about the incident. The reason some people can get away with this is that there is not the slightest possibility they are acting. If you are not acting, then you are cold, deadly serious—and he was. No one ever knew how many people he killed, but then he is still out there and perhaps the list continues to grow. I suppose if there is a positive to come out of such raw aggression, it's that at least he was on our side, whatever that means. I am respectful of such men as I know they have little choice in how they act. As with the shark, there are times when nature simply produces the perfect killing machine and in a sense that is almost beautiful. If not beautiful, then something deserving of respect and deference. To forget that may well be the last thing you ever do.

We would practice "Aggressive Preventive Patrol," which for all its complexity means driving around at night with the windows down and being observant. You don't have to look far for crime and with any luck it will almost certainly find you. Most police respond after a crime has been committed and find the who's who, then in good course the courts take over. The obvious failure of the system is that you need a victim before you have a crime and you need a crime before you can expect the police to become involved, a Catch-22. In our tough streets program we had a good solid team and worked to prevent crime by hitting the criminal before they could strike. Is this aggressive policing? Of course it is. We knew the neighborhood and we had our sources (snitches) so we often found ourselves at a crime scene before the criminals even showed. We played for keeps and assumed our adversaries did also. In diplomatic terms, we showed the flag, we spoke quietly, but we carried a big stick, (all the better to hit you with, my dear).

Going back to an earlier theme, nothing beats a thief catching a thief, and nothing quiets violence better then the threat or actuality of greater violence. One thing we had in our various small police groups and later in advanced communication technology, was backup just around the corner or a call away. The thugs we were up against might consider themselves tough, but no one was tougher than our gang: Man for man, we had the smarts, the guns, the authority and-most important-the desire to deliver the greatest damage for the buck. The real division, though, was experience and organization. We had been there before for many years and knew what we were about, and if we found ourselves in over our heads, we could call out the Cavalary. It's not an exaggeration made for TV or movies that if a cop was in danger every other cop would drop what he was doing and rush at breakneck speed to the officer's assistance. If a cop was in the middle of a burglary (his own), he would stop the break-in and speed to the aid of a brother in need. If a cop was killed, there would not be a stone on the planet the killer could hide under and, when caught, chances are the killer would not live to see his day in court. There was no margin allowed for cop killers.

This all goes back to the fractured nature of our existence. It was not be a cop, be a crook, be a cop, be a crook: In practice, we often did both at the same time and saw little conflict in it. If the natural order of the world is this way, why should an individual find it wanting? Again, it was your choice whether or not to remain a cop, but you knew, all knew, that one man could not change the system and it would be foolhardy to try. Fight them or join them, and there was never really a choice. You looked after yourself, your family, your extended family (the force), and then the public, and to do this you conformed to the status quo. You participated or not as you and the situation dictated, but one thing you never did was to outwardly question or scheme to change what was; that would be a fool's errand and a very dangerous pursuit. If you couldn't live with it, leave: If you stayed, just shut up, do your job and count your blessings (and extra income). When possible, the rule was, 10s and 20s with no consecutive serial numbers. Leave the peanuts for the monkeys and keep the big bucks for yourself. What you don't want is for one monkey to stop the show, which in police jargon means don't screw everything up for everyone by having a minor player get greedy.

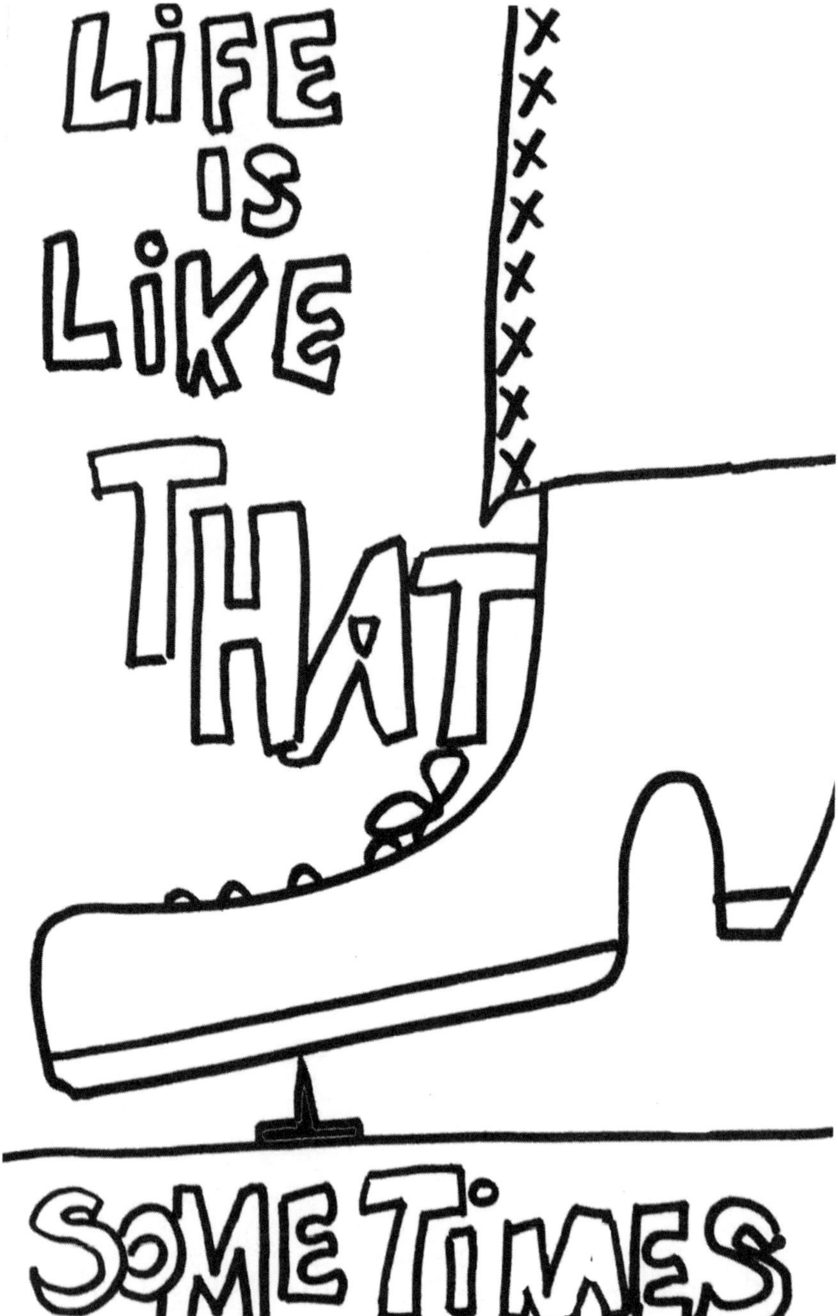
LIFE
IS
LIKE
THAT
SOMETIMES

Chapter 13

There are seminal moments in everyone's life, and for a cop it's no different. For me, the moment of truth came as a rookie while eating at a diner during my lunch break.

I was sipping coffee when I noticed two funny looking characters come through the front door. Not funny in a Bozo the Clown way, just acting cautious and looking a bit seedy. The seedy part is fine by me, but the cautious looks around set off some alarms. They sat down a few booths from me.

I walked over to the other table and asked one of the guys if I could speak with him outside, telling the other guy to stay where he was. I told the cook to call in for an assist as we had no portable radios in the mid-60s and I had a hunch this this guy was a wanted felon mentioned in the daily bulletin. The cook never called this in since I had already paid my tab. The first guy got up and we went outside to my patrol vehicle. I had the guy stand by my car while I started it up. It was cold outside and our radios needed to heat up before they could be used. As I returned to the fellow, he swung around and pointed a gun at me, a Five shot .38 Caliber Rhome snub nose revolver. He pulled the trigger again and again. He was close enough that I could read the engraving on the side of the gun and he shot five times from maybe five feet away. He missed, five times. He took off running, with me in close pursuit. He ran all over the place, jumped parked cars, ran through traffic (which is both dangerous and against the law) and up an alley. I knew this alley and pulled my revolver and fired, the first shot nearly taking my head off. The sound was so terrific from the .357 Mag in that concrete canyon that it took out my hearing. My other shots were closer but still missed. The shooter reloads and is around 5'4" and is jumping back and forth like a madman, firing all the time. He shoots five more times. I reload and return fire and missed six times. The guy ran up a flight of stairs and tried to reload his revolver. I threw my empty gun at him and drove my shoulder into his middle. He went up against the wall and I picked him up and threw him over the safety rail and heard him hit two stories below. When the investigators arrived, they questioned the need for throwing him over the rail. I responded that it seemed like the right thing to do at the time, but I had them repeat their comments so many times due to my new hearing disorder that they eventually lost interest in the question. They then asked how I knew there was a trash dumpster below that he would hit and bounce off and I said that was news to me.

The guy was carted away and was in serious condition at the hospital for some time. I returned to the diner and the fellow's partner was still sitting in the booth he had occupied earlier. I have no idea why he didn't leave, but he was also arrested. Turned out these crooks escaped from a Federal Pen and wanted to pull off an armed robbery. They were casing the restaurant when this all began.

The next day Captain O'Connor asked to see me in his office. I knocked and entered and he had me close the door. This is before department shrinks so he does just like in the movies. He opens the bottom drawer on his desk and pulls out a bottle. He gives me a glass and takes one for himself. He says, "Nice work yesterday with that punk, yeh, nice work." We each have our drink and as I rise, he says, "Hey, kid, take the rest of the day off, but I expect you back here tomorrow morning. By the way, why don't you hit the range and improve a bit on your shooting?"

Chapter 14

There is something about reality that holds no resemblance to film or television. I was considered a formidable presence and had the respect, so to speak, of those I served with. This high profile landed me choice assignments undercover and on special tactical or response units.

I was working the night shift with my Sergeant and a couple of other officers and we were all dressed in civies. There had been a rash of late night holdups and snatch and runs on the West Side, the bad side of town. We were, for lack of a better descriptive, cruising for a brusin; We wanted to let the street thugs know that doing this in Mayor Daley's city had its consequences and that we were acting under one of those famous or infamous-directives from City Hall to correct the problem and not be on the news. How we did it was up to us. The idea of such patrols is to simply lower all the windows and cruise slowly in places most reasonable people would avoid.

So here we were, driving at 2 a.m. in deserted streets, when I look over at a closed gas station and see a large, older model pimpmobile with three dudes in it speeding away. As they did, they jumped the curb and sparks flew from the underside. I was driving, so the chase was on. This was a classic movie chase if everthere was one, up one street, down another, on the sidewalk, high speed scrapes of walls and parked cars. These guys really wanted to get away. We were undercover so we didn't have a gumball machine but we did hit the siren. We are whaling down Congress Parkway when the thugs fucked up and turned into an industrial area. I was familiar with this area and knew there was no good way out. All you could do was dodge loading docks, trash dumpsters and empty crates. This is no place for the Indy 500 as these idiots were to find out. They go into a long side skid on hitting some oil or water and slide to a stop by a loading dock. The driver jumps out to run and I leap out of our car instantly (I don't even know if it was stopped all the way, but that's show biz).

I was armed with a revolver that was hardly standard issue, a Smith and Wesson 41 Magnum six inch. This gun is much more powerful that a .357 Magnum which in turn is much more powerful than the standard issue .38 Special. A 41 Mag will put a bullet through an engine block, so it has no problems at all with people. I was young and thought bigger was better, but with experience I have come to change my mind some on that.

The driver was sprinting away. I identified myself and yelled for him to stop. He turned and pulled a revolver from his pants and shot at me so I leveled my gun and fired back. The noise was like an ice pick shoved into my ear and caused a sharp pain and intense ringing in my head. I had also not seated the gun comfortably in my hand so the sharp recoil triggered nerves from my palm all the way up my arm. I felt the shot going out, but the guy I shot was not so lucky. The bullet, traveling at around 2400 feet per second, slammed into his right shoulder and instantly passed right through. The shock wave behind the bullet, something never mentioned on TV or in film, followed the slug and enlarged the hole several times and caused terrible damage. In westerns, the good guy always shoots the bad guy in the shoulder and all that happens is that the fellow in the black hat clutches his shoulder and says, "You got me, Sheriff."

In the real world, the bullet obliterated the rotator cuff and shoulder joint, splintered bone and cut through major arteries. The guy just dropped, again different then film. In the entertainment industry, a shot will throw the person being hit several feet backwards, right off their feet; in real life, you just drop like a bag of wet newspapers. I came over to him and kicked his gun away and knelt down. If you have ever smelled real violence, you never forget it. The great quantity of blood, spurting out with each heartbeat had made a large pool, and hot blood smells like something metallic. His blood mixed with the dirt and oil on the asphalt. Some seeped in, but most just stayed on the surface, and in that light it almost looked black. He had lost all bodily control so that was also present; it smelled like death. He was dazed and looked right into my eyes and said, "You just killed this nigger." I will never forget those words. The wound was fatal and his struggling a few moments later just quickened the end.

It was ugly and I felt... nothing. I stood and looked around at the emptiness of the scene, smelled the early moist cold air, turned my head around to clear the ringing and I still felt... nothing. My arm still ached from the recoil.

As described earlier, the other two guys in the car were also armed. My partner in the Tactical Unit, Jim Humphrey, walked up to the car and took out his revolver and stated for all to hear, "I am going to waste these guys." Sarg just stepped aside: Jim was going to do whatever he wanted and would go through anyone, ANYONE who stood in his way. I walked up to him and said evenly "Hey, look, good idea, I like it, but this is not the place or time. Think about it, one killing already, and three would make for a really bad mess." Jim acknowledged the wisdom of my input and backed off-for one of the few times in his life. That I had just taken a life moments before may have swung the argument in my favor. I had made my point.

I had just taken a life and felt nothing. With my Sarg riding shotgun and witnessing the entire event, there was no question it would go down as a "Righteous shooting" so no problem on that count. The higher-ups in the Department wanted to keep it all on the quiet as not to inflame race relations. Thus, it got little mention in the local papers or on TV.

I aged a lot that day and not all for the better. I've had a hard time explaining my emotions on this to anyone and the department didn't have shrinks on staff to help out in cases like this. You just sucked it up and reported to work the next day. I couldn't sleep for several days and was both excited and shocked at what I had done, what I felt I had to do. I had taken a human life and it wouldn't be the last, but for one person, all his tomorrows ended that day and now he was nothing more than dead flesh and bone at the City Morgue.

I've gone over it so many times in my head and the outcome is always the same. I don't care how good a shot you are, until you are doing it in anger, for real, on a city street, you just don't know. It's not glamorous, not exciting, not a good feeling, but also not a bad one; life is life and death is death. So I lived that day and the one died, both choices we made. By the way, anyone who would think or suggest I might have shot the gun out of his hand might keep in mind I was aiming for his body mass (middle) and hit his upper shoulder, so someone is watching way too much television.

But that's death in the big city. It doesn't even merit a mention in the local papers. So you wonder just how much one life is worth and the answer sometimes is nothing, nothing at all. I also learned that to really taste life you need to cheat death. This is something big game hunters know. Risk-taking skiers and divers also know, and now I knew it, too... I was shocked by what had transpired, but thrilled that I had responded instantly and had prevailed; Pandora's Box was now open.

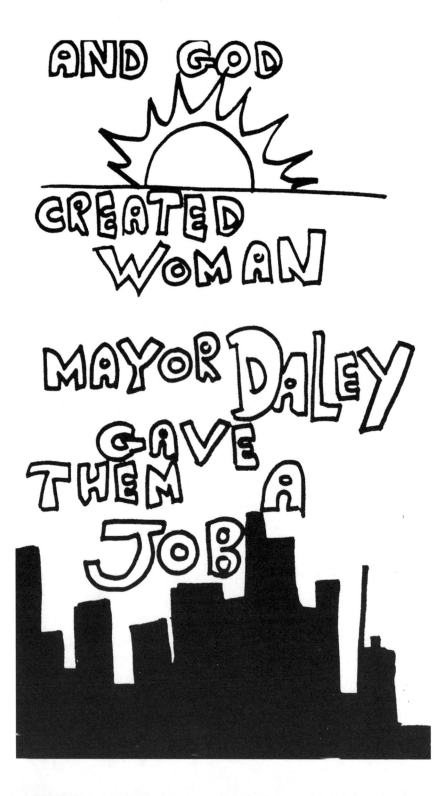

Chapter 15

I am a chauvinistic pig, oink oink, but you probably have guessed this by now. I suspect most cops who started in the old system and then had to transition to the new could be counted as such.

Women on the force simply had to happen; it was written in the stars and mandated by the Mayor. Make no mistake, this was not a social experiment, this was going to happen and this was going to succeed.

The force began to change around 1970. Sure there were women in policing before this; they were called matrons and worked the jails and a few specialty areas. But after it was so decreed, they occupied virtually all positions that existed and in time rose to command rank.

I've given this a great deal of thought and have come to the conclusion that women's introduction to the force is the point of change between the old system and what I would call new policing. The first women to join were a very focused group and cut across the range of talent and reason, but they were pioneers and had a very tough road to travel. There were the secretaries and waitresses to be sure, but many took pay cuts to join and were professional women (in a good way as in college educated) and saw this as the changing of the guard. There were no women firefighters at that time or women garbage collectors; this was their window of opportunity and they were up to the challenge.

Around 1970, there was Affirmative Action, but no Sexual Discrimination. These women had to take it. They were purposely partnered with males in the patrol cars and I don't mind saying it led to many awkward moments. Consider the late night stakeout: no more pissing into a empty milk carton. What are you going to talk about, joke about? "Hey, look at the rack on that one, or "With jugs like that," how can she keep from falling on her face, or maybe my face." You know what I mean; men and women simply cannot be friends under any condition or circumstance. That little thing sitting next to you all night starts to look pretty good at 4 a.m. and reaching for the cigarette lighter and brushing this or that, whether on purpose or not is, well, just is. Consider again the long, boring stakeout. Being simply honest here, when I wake up I often have a piss hard-on. Maybe it was a woody from a most excellent dream. All guys know you just can't control what you just can't control. On a few occasions, I fell asleep and my head ended up on the softest, most comfortable pillow I ever enjoyed. I hardly had to fluff it, but I did drool some. I will let your imagination go where it's headed and you would be right.

There is also the question of how far you can trust your new partner. Can someone without nuts get yours out of the fire, or do you have to do the work of two?

I may not be fair in this, but it's not a civics experiment or philosophy debate, it's my life and I am rather protective of it. I have to say that in my time on the force, policewomen did not let me down any more than the guys, but if I were assigned one as a partner on patrol tomorrow, I would honestly still have my reservations.

Wives were also unhappy in that these woman cops were spending more time with their husbands than they were. And, frankly, they knew their husbands and that this might be just too much temptation. Further, the welfare of the family depended on the father's income since most wives did not work, leading to great concern on the part of the wives that their husbands' safety may be on the line. They didn't care for that either.

There were instances of fire fights when the women didn't draw their weapons. In an incident where I was personally involved, the rush to success of women on the street came into sharp focus for me. The Old Italian neighborhood had not seen a traffic ticket issued ever, at least not since the cow incident with Mrs. O'Leary. One day, a one man (woman) patrol went to that area and this young woman cop starts writing tickets. A call comes in to dispatch that you had better get some "Guys" over there right away-your officer is in serious trouble. Apparently more than one motorist was less than pleased at seeing a ticket being put on their windshield for double parking. "What the fuck you think you are doin?" "Writing you a ticket for double parking." "Like fuckin' hell you are." I was the first officer to respond and this guy greets me as I exit my car and quietly hands me her gun, her ticket book and her shirt. He says "Get her the fuck out of here and nobody had ever better write tickets in our neighborhood." I got her out of her cuffs, out of her car and out of Dodge. No more tickets were written in Little Italy. She got off easy.

In bar fights that teams of partnered women cops responded to, it was not unusual that when backup arrived, the bartender handed the responding officers their guns, held for safekeeping.

Back to the sexual tension. If a female cop had two legs, two arms, a head and boobs, she was either a target of the guys, or if she were not interested, then she was a lesbian. If on an individual basis respect was shown by a male cop, the female would be down his throat saying she wanted to be treated just like the guys. But when she was treated just like the guys, well, it just wasn't well received.

Later problems arose when some of these women gained command rank and the male officers had to take orders or criticism from them. I can tell you that never went down well.

Like I said, this was never an experiment; it was going to work and work it did. I realize in retrospect it did something else. The women on the force didn't universally sign up to the illegal sideshow that was the all male department before. They were focused and intent on changing things and one of the things they changed was how everyone eventually behaved. Not only did the manners and demeanor improve over time, but the shenanigans became much less center stage, with mostly the really serious players still participating in illegal activities. It was like having your mother along for the ride, or your sister; things just changed. At the same time, things like portable communications devices made the scene, as well as other modern tools of law enforcement. It was a brave new day.

I think it's like computers are today. If you were born before the computer age, computers are a challenge. If you were born after the computer age of enlightenment, you work computers as a natural extension of your mind and body.

I will always be an old War Horse, at least as it pertains to policing, and I just can't help it. I have to admit it was and is for the best and that women make great cops, fantastic investigators and can resolve situations in better ways than breaking skulls, but there are still things men do better. Walk into a redneck bar full of drunks and you had better be a big guy with a big stick (know what I mean) or you may just become part of the evening's entertainment. I must say, there are women as strong as some men, but they are the exception to the rule.

Being a student of unconventional law enforcement, I championed tools and techniques before they became widely recognized and used. For example I became very proficient in the Martial Arts. It's not that I objected to shooting the bad guys, but sometimes even the most enjoyable things in life, if done to excess, can become humdrum. In other words, there are times that due to circumstance or choice a good chop is better than a loud bang. I was known as a very accomplished practitioner of the Eastern arts (and I am not talking about watercolor in New Jersey).

One day, I received an urgent call from my Captain who asked if he could pick me up and take me to the site of a serious situation, one the department wanted to keep out of the news. He drives up and has me hop in his squad car. This is very unusual as he seldom chooses to leave the comfort of the station and I was undercover, and let's say not suited for mainstream police work at the moment. As he drives, he tells me that a recent graduate from the Academy has gone bonkers and was holding his wife at gunpoint in their apartment. When we pulled up and pounded a few flights of stairs, I see the hallway lined with the city's finest, guns drawn. They could have taken on an army, but that begs the question of how many cops it takes to screw in a light bulb, and I'd prefer not to go there. My Captain says "Gary, everyone knows you are a lights out kung fu expert or something, so we want you to kick in the door over there and disarm the guy before he can plug his wife." "Ah Cap," I responded, "I don't think that is such a great idea." "Why not?" "Well, for one thing, because I will probably get shot." "So what do you suggest?"

I asked if anyone there had been in the Academy with our guy and two knockout female rookies come forward. They looked great in their uniforms, and you could just tell not much would be lost without their official blues. I said "Look ladies, this guy isn't talking and that's a real bad sign, so I want the one of you who knows him best to go up to the door (well to the side of the door) and call in to him and start a conversation." One of the women says she knows him pretty well and will try. Up to the door she goes, with 20 officers on both sides of her in the dimly lit hallway. You could cut the tension and just knew you were about to hear a scream and a thunderous sound. All were hushed; you could hear the breathing.

She yells in, "Hey John, this is Betty, remember me from the Academy, how you doing, guy?" "Who?" he yells back, "I don't remember you." Now this is getting dicey so I step up and yell in the door, "Hey, she's the one with the really big tits," to which John says, "Yeh, I do remember you," and as he opens the door, he is quickly taken into custody. Everyone, except Betty, was having a hoot over this and once more my quick wit kept my ass and the rest of me out of the line of fire. We rescued the wife, secured the scene, got a good laugh and Betty got a nickname she would carry for the rest of her career. Sometimes you just have to go with your gut and holler out the obvious, and this time it worked.

You know how I feel about women in police work and most specifically if they are my partner, but I have to admit there was one notable exception to the rule.

Late in my career I had to work "a day in lieu of," which meant that once more I was in hock for some violation of something. Rather than lose a day's pay, I could work it off by "Contributing" a free day's work. Wow, what a concept. It was Saturday night and I found myself in a Beat Car for the midnight shift. This just griped my cookies to no end. I was teamed with Maggie McGuire. It was 1986, and she was one of the original "Babes on the block" or first Policewomen. She was an original; mid 30s, small, very attractive and very assertive. Turns out she was the current girl pal of my old friend Art (Superman) so I cut her more slack than usual. I have to say most policewomen go to seed after a time on the force. They just don't handle those donuts as well as their male counterparts, but not Maggie. Art was finished with his fourth or fifth marriage by that time, but that they were fond of each other brought instant credibility on my part; they were good people.

She was driving, one because she wanted to and two, because I didn't give a shit. I thought I could catch some zzz's, but Maggie had other ideas. She was making traffic stops right and left for the smallest infraction: broken tail light, broken headlight, cracked windshield, etc. She was just so damn competitive. We had maybe ten of these stops and she was shoving people, slamming them up against the sides of their cars. I was the good cop to her bad cop (a new role for me, obviously). We get a call of a domestic at Montrose Avenue and respond. I ask her if we want a backup and she says no, we can handle it. We trek up to the second floor landing of the apartment building and knock on the door. Said door opens and there stands this mountain of a man, clad in nothing but shorts and a white hard hat. This guy in his Fruit of the Looms and construction helmet says he is the meanest, toughest, strongest SOB there is, and this offends me since I am partnered with a fucking woman and don't appreciate such language. I had this feeling the shit was going to hit the fan big time.

Communications were with portable radios, which I carried since Maggie had been the designated driver. I said again to her, "Let's call in for backup," and she nodded. I made the call from the hall, but was advised all cars were tied up and to do the best we could and they would send someone when free. This guy, who looked like that construction worker for the Village People, but was as large as the entire group, wouldn't budge. His wife would not come out of the locked bathroom even with us there, so we were at an impasse. Women tend to make better negotiators, so Maggie gave it a try, but nothing. As she was doing this, I looked around the room without moving and noticed gouges in doors and walls, overturned furniture and the like. This fuck kept saying how physically adept he was, how strong and invincible; he was his own fan club. We were now approaching a half hour on this call, and along with the other shit of the evening, I was starting to boil over. I made a last fruitless attempt at compromise by asking him if he could go somewhere else for the night while we sorted things

out, but he would have none of that. "It's my house
and I'm not leaving."

I had known for the past 15 minutes this was
not going to end well and was waiting for the right
time to act. Remember that I don't like to engage in
any fight I don't know for certain I can win. I make
a fist out of eyesight and smash this fucker right in
his nose and flatten it to the level of the rest of his
face. He goes flying right into the hall and lands
on his back. I hit him with all the pent-up energy
and anger that the whole damn fucking evening has
piled on me; I could not have put more force into
that punch. It lifted him right off his feet. But, true
to his word, he was one tough motherfucker. I move
to the hall to cuff him and though dazed, he gets to
his knees when I kick him full in the gut with all my
might and he flies down the flight of stairs and ends
up on the first floor landing. Out of the corner of
my eye, I see Maggie with her mouth open and jaw
dropped.

I move to cuff him, and he tries to get up. I
kick him once again with my steel toed boots and
he flies down to the lobby this time. He is dazed
and bloody, and I cuff him and throw him into the
cage part of our car and slam the door. Maggie is
standing there, but she doesn't say a word. I tell her
to get the wife and to take her to the station, and—if
she refuses—we will lock her up, too. I call dispatch and say we won't be needing the backup and
that we are on our way in.

When we get there, as is proper procedure, the

lockup keeper refuses our prisoner. Nobody can be booked that is physically "Damaged" without first going to Emergency. Paramedics are called, and this fucker is transported. While this was taking place, Maggie was with the wife and told her if she didn't sign the complaint Maggie would mop the floor with her face; she signed. I found out later our construction worker was hospitalized for over two weeks with numerous broken bones and damaged organs and other internal injuries. This SOB files Police Brutality charges against us, both State and Federal. I am called downtown later for a statement and a run down of exactly what had taken place. I first asked to hear what the guy had said and it turns out he said he had been beaten unmercifully by 5' 3" Maggie. He was that afraid of me, so he would rather say little Maggie busted his chops. We were exonerated.

Maggie later told Art that she had never seen such an awesome display of power in her life; it was Superman she said this to. I was more than happy to let her have the credit for the thrashing as it only added to her reputation and I didn't need the publicity, though everyone in the Station knew the truth. Oh yes, the last thing I said to the construction worker before closing the car door on him, I asked him if he wanted his hard hat.

Chapter 16

Alexander Dumas wrote the classic *Tale of Two Cities* about the changing times in France, particularly Paris at the time of the French Revolution. It is a story of two worlds that exist in the same time in the same place, but which are worlds apart. They come into violent conflict and one world almost completely consumes the other. It is a time of profound loss, destruction and pain, but also a story of rebirth and noble thought and action.

I was thinking they could almost have been talking about Chicago in '68. In both instances, the gathered masses demanded to be heard, were through taking direction from the old establishment and wanted their voices to resonate throughout the land. What really caught my attention is that in France during the French Revolution the call to arms was LIBERTE', and from this comes our concept of liberty. Further along this line of thought, the Statue of Liberty in New York was a gift from France to the United States in acknowledgment of our declaration to be the home of all peoples who desired freedom. The youth and underclass of France proclaimed that it was time to abolish the monarchy and to install representative government, and the youth of America, those who fight our wars and pay the price, stood up and said "no more," we demand a say in how the future is drawn and we will no longer simply follow the prescribed direction without study and discussion.

It may be a stretch, but I view Chicago before '68 and after as a parallel to France and their revolution. In both case, the status quo was shattered and change resulted.

At the time one doesn't, of course, see the greater meaning of the event one is participating in. As a cop or a protester, your focus is hard on what may present the greatest immediate danger to you. We were all aware of examples elsewhere in the country of what happens when polar opposites come together; Kent State is one such example. It is not a game and people can and do die, this is for real. All birth comes from pain and, in the case of Chicago and the U.S., the rebirth was pain. However, what happened in Chicago was induced and not natural. Would such change have happened anyway? Who knows, but I suspect the answer is yes, its time had come. That I was breathing the same air as all the participants, that I saw what they saw, felt what they felt, makes me believe I am party to history's birth, the rebirth of our nation.

It is thought that the Revolutionary War started at the North Bridge by mistake or miscalculation, but in the end it was from our point of view, the correct course, albeit for perhaps the wrong reasons. The riots and conflicts the nation and world witnesses firsthand in Chicago in '68 were perhaps the same. Certainly there was intent on both sides to come to and participate in the dance, but I doubt anyone had any idea where it would lead. So once more the correct outcome resulted from what may well have been a poorly thought out start.

In the end, as all Americans know, it's the results that count. Our nation today was reformed in the flames and screams of Chicago, and I was there.

Chapter 17

Politics in Chicago 1966 go back farther than 1860s and may even predate Mrs. O'leary's cow (look it up). Parts of New York City were run in a similar manner, but "Chicago was the city that worked."

In Chicago for over 100 years, few people other than building inspectors and department heads made good money; most everyone else got by with much less. Two things were important, 1) that you had a good, secure position (pension) and 2) that you supported all those who were supporting you. Hence the machine.

It was felt better to have many people suckling at the public teat than to have widespread poverty and unemployment. Your job was important; it was "yours" and needed protection. If the boss, Mayor Daley, said everyone needed to vote in a certain way, a few bucks would be spent to be certain that happened—and it always happened. A joke maybe, but Mayor Daley is credited with the saying, "Vote early and often." It was known that most dead people in Chicago voted for the mayor no matter who was running (the last time they took a straw poll, it came in almost 2 to 1 in favor of the Mayor's choice).

Patronage and cronyism, were the two cornerstones of Chicago politics. It was never about what you knew and always about whom you knew. As an example, lets look at my Sergeant, the one who lived down the block and got me into the academy. He had eight kids and the Church felt he had to cut things a little too close. So out of the blue the man in blue gets a promotion to Sergeant. Things always happened for a reason in Chicago, and things were never as they appeared to be on the surface. It was a complicated life, remembering who you shared confidences with, keeping stories straight, knowing who in the leadership of the department was a 90-day no hit wonder, who had made his bones and who belonged to the Other Mob at the same time. This is one very complicated game and there was no program to tell you who was who. A real problem a rose when someone transferred in from another District, from the outside entirely or came directly from the Academy. You had to be very cautious in feeling the guy out for his willingness to engage in those alternative revenue sources I mentioned.

Not that Internal Affairs was ever all that effective in Chicago and, in fact, they had their own scams going, but maybe there was a state or national taskforce to root out the problem (us) of which we were unaware. The one thing we always had going for us was that we shared our Code of Blue. We belonged, in essence, to the same Fraternity, and were fiercely protective. In our world what we were doing was the norm and it was also tradition that if you were a cop, you were also a crook. The only thing that was not well accepted was anyone who might upset the apple cart. If you were going to stay in the system and you played ball, all would be well and life would be good. It wasn't only Chicago cops who knew this; the politicians knew it and to some extent so did the general public. Protection and law enforcement costs, pure and simple, and the community teat just doesn't provide adequate nourishment to support the force.

Our days were divided into three categories. First, there was "Business as usual" when you go on patrol, do the minimum of work possible, arrest someone for show and chalk it up as another good day. Then there is "Didn't see that coming," which is a day that starts out fine and then goes south, such as being involved in a multiple homicide or stopping a bank robbery in progress and the like. The good thing about these days is that they go by pretty fast and you get to feel like a cop. Finally, there are the "Ah, shit" days, which would include all riots, national conventions and wide scale mayhem. A crash at O'Hare would fall into this category. Certain things were important. Know your Captain and do him a favor now and then so your transfer, when it comes, might not be to a station just this side of Ice Station Alaska. Get to know and befriend the secretary and the Desk Sergeant and, most important of all, get to really know your partner. Your life and your future is in that persons hands so be sure they have your six and are loyal. If not, you may as well put that lead in your brain box now and save the trouble of doing it later; your partner is that important.

There are a few general rules that seem universal. Those who talk a lot about something have probably never done that something. What is damaging about breaking the law is getting caught, so in this line of thought, nobody but the people themselves know who the most successful criminals are. Don't get caught.

In Chicago police talk and Mob, they would say, "How did the fish get caught? By opening its mouth."

Back to the workings of the city, At its core was the Mob or Outfit. The First Ward was, and has been shown to have been, run by Made Members of the Mob. This was in the most influential ward in the city. This iteration of the Mob was said to be considerably stronger than that which existed during Capone and Prohibition. This Mob was sophisticated and organized, and was recognized as arguably the most powerful Mob in the U.S. at that time. They had influence or controlling influence in the unions, police, politicians and all public services. To do anything illegal or off color in Chicago in that time required payment of a street tax, and to not pay bought you a one way ticket to the trunk of a car parked at Chicago O'Hare. The Mob was the tie that binds, and even the courts were in their deep pockets; they worked with immunity.

THE SUMMER OF DISCONTENT

Chapter 18

"T"he Projects" rather sounds like something the Army Corps. of Engineers might do, but this is different. In an attempt to clean up the city, some smart person had the idea of building high-rises and using them for low income housing. Good idea, bad result. If you put all the poor and disenfranchised in one place, you end up with a place that is both poor and disenfranchised, and from this comes poor upkeep, gangs and concentrated crime. This also makes for places the police will not go unless there is no other choice.

Winters in Chicago due to the affect of the lake, are miserable but as noted before, you don't get riots when it's cold and miserable. However, hot and miserable is something else entirely. When its cold, people obviously stay inside, but hot and no air means everyone is on their porch or outside. The inside of these buildings were stinking, sweltering vertical hells. Most cops in Chicago in the 60s and 70s were white, so if something went down at the Projects, it came to us to ferret out the evil-doers. I don't care who you are, you'd have to be a complete psycho to chase anyone into one of those buildings; they made the Alamo look like good odds. In one instance, some moron at headquarters assigned two cops to foot patrol at the Projects, and they were gunned down by a shooter. The sniper fire was so bad, it took considerable time to retrieve the bodies which weighed heavily on us.

One hot, oppressive late spring day, it finally happened—open warfare. The spark that set it off was the assassination of Dr. Martin Luther King. Following that event, there was simply too much steam in the engine and something had to give. Here you have low-no income towers standing some 15 stories tall, arranged around a green (Brown more precisely), and shots were being fired. This project was walking distance from Michigan Avenue and the Gold Coast (Lake Front), which was City Center. The rioting was leaving the projects and threatening to move to the high-end areas so it was decreed this a line be drawn and that this incursion would simply not happen. It would end where it was and go no further.

The word went out citywide; all leaves and vacations were cancelled, all hands had to report- and bring weapons. It was all over the news so we knew what was happening, but not how out of control it was. We grabbed whatever we had around and headed to our stations for assignment. What a ragtag, motley crew, the original dirty (several) dozen. We gathered in the squad room and looked like some underground army from hell. Some of us had shotguns, some deer rifles. Others had knives, and there was at least one sword and a spear. Understand this was before SWAT so even the Chicago Police Department was not equipped for this kind of wide scale unrest and violence. Deputy Superintendent Lindsky took one look at us and said with disgust, "I can't send you guys out there looking like that!" to which we said "Fine, then we'll just take our shit and go home." "No, you take yourselves and your shit to the Projects and stay off the news." We drove anything that moved to the Projects and came under fire a block before we got to our destination. This was out of a whacked out movie, but the bullets were real and we for sure did not have the high ground. We crouched behind our cars and traded fire with people on balconies. An officer beside me had a Lugar his dad had brought back from Germany (his dad was a German officer in the Second World War) and was trying to figure out how to load the damn thing. This finally accomplished, he took aim and pulled the trigger and the gun blew up. We had a good laugh over that. This one shit around ten stories up was keeping us pinned down when a car sped up with a hunting rifle with a scope that could see Martians on Mars from Chicago, sticking out the back window. The car stopped suddenly and a second later there is this terrific crack and the mope on the tenth floor simply disappeared—like he was there and then all that was there was a mist of red droplets. We all thought there would be at least one vacancy at the projects after today and the day wasn't even half over.

One famous or infamous occurrence that took place during this riot happened on the West side. There was one station in the middle of that area called the 11th District (Fillmore), informally known as Fort Apache. When the insurrection happened citywide it was most intense in the 11th. Phone lines were cut, streets blocked and the radio knocked off the air. The officers of Fort Apache were pinned down by random gun fire and precise sniper fire. They were running out of food, water was cut off and they felt, correctly, that they had been abandoned and thrown to the wolves. Bullets had penetrated all the windows, the doors had been shot out, an unsuccessful attempts made to torch the place. Office furniture and filing cabinets were pushed against any opening. The fighting went on day and night. The pent-up rage that boiled over on one side met the hostility that came from neglect and indifference on the police side. Fort Apache became one of many symbols for institutional indifference and neglect.

In point of fact, it took days for the Department at large to even discover that there was a problem and then to do something about it. Out of sight, out of mind, but then the city was in flames and chaos reigned. This could easily have been the darkest blotch on the otherwise sullied reputation of the Chicago PD and on Chicago at large. This incident has not, to my knowledge, ever been truthfully or accurately recounted and is simply another uncomfortable tidbit lost in the dust bin of history.

Back to my marvelous adventure. We were running this way and that, firing from the hip and zigzagging like we knew what we were doing. It was about as much fun as any of us had ever had. One thing that was obvious in all such confrontations, be it the '68 Convention a few months later or this riot, there was never any police line management on the scene. The bigwigs were out of sight, out of sound and out of danger, and we had to improvise without much leadership. A Sergeant on the scene came over and yelled, "Who is in charge here?" We yelled back "Hey, that would be you." When the sun set, you could see tracer rounds and sparks where our bullets were hitting the sides of the buildings. It was quite a light show seeing those phosphorus tipped rounds arcing up to the higher windows and balconies and then playing back and forth like a garden hose if fired in rapid succession. One little difference was that where a stream from a garden hose can put out a fire, our tracers were starting them all over the place. Must have been quite a sight flying into O'Hare that evening; Chicago looked like Beirut. The unrest and violence was citywide, but I can only speak of the area I was involved with.

You can only have so much fun and then mommy calls you home for dinner, so with ammo low and our heads hurting from all the noise, we decided to call it a day. That seemed to get it out of everyone's system and only a few people were killed. Since this was Chicago, a few people were always killed each day, Except now much of the West Side was burning!

We, as a Department, started to set up contingency plans after that so in the future we would have a more unified and strategic approach to the problem, but in the summer of '68 it was "Bar the door and hand me over that fire stick."

The one thing that I came away with was the insight that if you haven't anything to live for it doesn't take a lot of reason to find something to die for. So we were the Law and Order but, honestly, Law had little to do with anything that day and order was nowhere to be found.

The '68 Convention in Chicago didn't just happen, it was meant to happen. Is this to say everything was choreographed? No. Is this to say the steps were put in motion and that this fed off of national and world events that same year and the answer is yes. No one knew where the conflagration once ignited would go and, honestly, no one really cared. The chips would fall where they may and in the process would reshape our nation and our way of life. Following is a brief history of the events of that year which fed the fire and guaranteed an occurrance of epic proportions and import.

This is what was happening in the U.S. and around the world prior to the convention.

Vietnam was going poorly and the images flashed to everyone's television set showed the reality of war as never before. The Tet Offensive was beamed each day into homes, showing dead American servicemen and the street execution of a North Vietnamese insurgent. Almost 25,000 young men were being drafted into the armed forces every month and at this juncture around 19,000 Americans had already died in the war. In late March of 1968, Lyndon Johnson in a surprise announcement flatly stated he would not run, nor accept his party's nomination for president at the convention later that summer.

In a nine week stretch between April and June of 1968, both Martin Luther King and Bobby Kennedy were assassinated, both shot down at the prime of their lives. I remember thinking, "How much more of this can I and the Country, take?" It seemed the very ground was being yanked from under our feet. Who would be next, what would be next?

There were riots throughout Mexico that were likened to a revolution and threatened to tear that world apart. There was the Summer Olympics in Mexico City and while the games were kept quiet, some American Athletes protested with black gloved clenched fist upon receiving their awards. This proved provocative and an embarrassment for the people back home.

It seemed the world was in unrest and parts of the ceiling kept falling wherever you looked.

Then came Chicago and a bad year turned chaotic. Whatever veneer of civilization had existed came off during the days leading up to the convention. Hostility bubbled to the surface almost like a volcanic event, but the pressure kept building. Nerves were rubbed bare in that fateful year, as each event unfolded, each more catastrophic than the last, and there was no end in sight. The very fabric of our great nation was starting to tear in all directions and the civility and shared values that had held us together were coming apart at the seams. Where there had been order and tradition, anarchy and disillusionment now stood. It would take only a little stone tossed upon the pile to topple everything when Mayor Daley delivered a giant dump truck (Teamster driven) and sent the whole fucking mess over the side and into oblivion.

Ours was a very old department in which I was one of the youngest. Most of my fellow officers were vets of past wars and took a very dim view of hippies or anyone in long hair and tie dye. From late spring up to the Convention, we experienced almost weekly demonstrations against the war and against the police. In fact, there was a 10,000 person demonstration on Michigan Avenue specifically against the police prior to September. As cops, we were as uncertain and uncomfortable as anyone else. Our carefully crafted world was getting turned on its head, and every day, every news report only went to unsettle the apple cart all the more. When the shit hit the fan or the fan hit the shit, what happened was a venting of tension, uncertainty and fear, fear of the unknown. Our boys were dying in great numbers in Southeast Asia, our finest athletes were protesting their own country in a country essentially at war, two of our brightest stars for the future were extinguished within weeks of each other and invitations were sent out to come to beautiful Downtown Chicago and mingle with your friends as the world burns. We all knew it was going to be a great gathering, one to tell your kids about, and maybe there would be door prizes.

Anyway, in most every way, 1968 was a very bad year, but one that changed the world.

THE 68 CONVENTION

Chapter 19

There are some people or events recognized solely by their name or a reference. Examples of this would be 1812 (The war), Bambino or the Babe, WWI or WWII and, I would add, the '68 Convention.

The '68 Convention refers to the 1968 Democratic Convention held in Chicago, which was in all ways "The perfect storm." The perfect storm is the confluence of all things in one place at one time, the coming together of all elements, the sum of every train in the world riding the intersecting lines of a pinwheel and all meeting at the point in the center at the same instant. The '68 Convention was such an event.

All things converged in space and time in an occurrence of biblical proportions in the week of the Democratic Convention, and it both defined our times, changed forever Chicago and the country. It became known as the quintessential label for the decade, a generation, and was the point of no return for a country at war, the start of the changing of the guard and the surrealistic climax of a grand show in the Theater of the Absurd. It was also how I met my wife.

Not to overstate it, but when an immovable object meets an irresistible force, something catastrophic and epic must happen, and it did.

THE IMMOVABLE OBJECT: Look it up

in your reference book; under Old School Political Machine you will find a stern picture of Mayor Richard J. Daley and a description of his "Political Machine," otherwise known as the Daley Machine and a reference to Chicago. It is instructive to consider that for most of the United States and the world, Chicago is the place that is known; Illinois is only the place where it is. Similarly, few people nationally would know who the schmuck is that is governor of the state, but everyone knows who the mayor of the city was; the city defines. I would call this the immovable object.

THE IRRESTIBLE FORCE: There are some things that simply cannot be denied. You don't ignore a hurricane (Lest at your own peril), a full eclipse of the sun, death, world war, the World Series or mile after mile of army ants slowly closing in on you from all sides. Some things are not to be ignored. The forces in play that week were hot passion over an unpopular war; a generation that demanded change and that did not recognize authority; a hot summer week with even higher humidity; a conscious effort to disenfranchise the protestors, provoke conflict and deny basic services; the world's eye; the world's press. This was the most important event of the decade. Mass hysteria on the part of the police and the city and numbers in the tens of thousands of protestors combined to create the Irresistible Force.

In astrological terms, this is the coming together of planetary bodies at incalculable speed, both insistent on occupying the same place in space at the same instant. What you get is an explosion of planet shattering magnitude and the creation of an entirely new solar system. That was the '68 National Convention in Chicago. This was an event of incalculable importance, the eye of the perfect storm, the climax of a decade, the defining moment of a century. This was the death of one world and the birth of the modern age, and I was there swinging a police baton (club) and not taking names. I was part of the Police Riot (as it became known), the tidal wave in blue that the world saw firsthand giving full measure of Daley Justice.

The first day of the Convention started weeks earlier with reports from the FBI and many other organizations and agencies that predicted with absolute authority and insistence that the protestors, with the world stage at hand, would use any and all tactics to disrupt and influence the Convention. In so doing, they would bring serious jeopardy to the force in Blue, the thin line separating the barbarians from the civilized. We were told we were going in harm's way and that we would be outnumbered, provoked, set up. Intelligence sources stated that the hippies, or Students for a Democratic Society, SDS or the Weathermen Underground, all militaristic outlawed terror organizations, were going to contaminate Chicago's water filtration plant by placing LSD in the water. That had us very concerned, yet at that point nothing would have surprised us. We fully expected to face a ruthless adversary that would think nothing of seeing us maimed, killed, subject to oven cleaner bombs, crap projectiles and all manner of insidious weapons of destruction. We were told clearly that we were going against an organized, trained and determined enemy that desired nothing less than absolute conflict and mayhem in front of news cameras. We, our men in Blue, were the sacrificial offering being put on the altar and that our only, our ONLY hope was to hit first, hit hardest and to take no prisoners. This would be absolute, no rules, no gloves, no quarter asked or given battle royal, that the clouds were gathering and the storm would arrive on schedule. We were wired tighter than those fine, skinny strings on the top of the guitar, we were pumped, armed and dangerous, and we intended to exact our pound of flesh and then just for the heck of it, continue to take pound after pound. Our instructions from our commanders was to the effect, do whatever you need to do and the only caution given was don't be caught on camera doing it. The Huns were at the gate and we were going to meet them on the proud fields (Parks actually) of the Windy City. It would be their blood that was spilled on the field and they, the protestors, would learn a simple but absolute lesson: No one comes to a party in Chicago that Mayor Daley throws without a fucking invitation. And as the good Mayor was heard saying about the men in Blue, "Our Police are not here to prevent disorder, our police are here to preserve disorder." He just had a way with words.

If ever there was a seminal moment, a sea of

change in America, it would have to be the 1968 Chicago Democratic Presidential Convention. The closest you can come to describing this confluence of causes and lifestyles is to say it was destiny.

On one side you had the lifestyle of the youth of the country who viewed with abject suspicion anything said by anyone over 30, and on the other side you had the establishment nationally and the "Machine" locally. It was *mano a mano,* and these two forces would be brought together for one week in a place of 95 degree heat with 95 per cent humidity and 100 per cent distrust.This could only result in a conflagration of biblical proportions—and then there was Mayor Daley.

Make no mistake about it, Chicago '68 was no accident, it was coldly on purpose and calculated on all sides. The agitators were practiced and worked with military precision and the police (myself included): were equally up to the task: unconditional, unrestricted warfare. We were told the only way to fight fire is with fire. We were going to be ready, and ready we were. Our orders came from on top, not from the White House, but from much higher— from Mayor Richard Daley himself. For us that meant anything goes and the results would justify the means.

We were practiced and ready for a showdown with the forces of evil, the protestors. This was the time of the Vietnam War, and this convention was the coming together of both sides of the equation: those who were forced by the draft to go and those doing the sending. The protestors might as well have been wearing black PJ's like the Viet Cong (VC) the way we saw them. We knew nothing like this had ever happened before in the U.S., and we were to learn years later that this was as bad as it ever gets.

That was our side of the story but I will add that it was a bit unnerving, being an officer of 22 years of age and facing protestors on the other side, also 22 years old. Very surrealistic.

As for the protestors, most were merely sheep, angry sheep maybe, but still just sheep. The core, the hard core were professional agitators who would make sure provocation was quickly at hand should television or news cameras be seen nearby.

The city didn't help things in how they laid out the rules of the convention. The city's main parks could be used during the day for protests and loitering, but would be closed by 11:00 p.m. every night and emptied. The protestors had absolutely no place to go when forced out of the parks by police and would simply roam the streets. It was terribly hot, sticky damp with no wind, and hot air blooming from the Convention Center itself. Like a tidal wave hitting the Poseidon, we came together time and time again. The protestors would hurl themselves against the police line protecting access to the Convention Center and we would push back, none too gently.

Something was always thrown, words screamed, and then the emotion would overflow and we had a riot. I did not say "the riot" since there were so many that it was a cluster riot. We would pour into the protestors' lines and use our clubs to beat some "sense" into those misguided youth while they used all sort of objects to similarly instill some "understanding" in us. A good time was had by all.

In one such encounter the lines broke and I was within the swirling mass of the protestors, swinging my club in a semi-circle to keep a little open space. This was hard, dirty, and dangerous work—and probably the most fun I had in recent memory. The rule was not to swing the club overhead but in an arc at body level (looked better on TV). I was wading through some humanity, knocking them down like bowling pins as I went when I was confronted by a lovely little hippie girl directly in front of me.

I thought maybe she needed an overhead and, as I raised my baton, I suddenly stopped and said, "Hey, you look familiar." She responded "Yeh, you do too. Were we in high school together?" "You're right, you are ......" and we had this most unusual surrealistic conversation in the middle of the mayhem. While we talked all other sounds receded and the riot around us went to slow motion. Finally, my arm was getting a little tired so I said, "Say, if you aren't doing anything after the riot, would you like to go out?" "Sure, sounds great." I got her phone number and later married her. I know what you are thinking. It was almost Neanderthal how I found my wife, but remember I never really did hit her with the club.

I know that last part, though true, will be considered a bit funny, but that was the only funny thing about those days. This was a clash of generations, the coming apart at the seams of the fabric America, the first time those fighting our wars stood up and said, "Shove it." It looked like the end of the world was at hand, but it is worth noting that those same people, those protestors are today's CEOs and high Government officials. I guess all you can really say is that growing up, either as an individual or a country, is a painful process—and you can't make an omelet without breaking some eggs. I broke quite a few eggs that week.

I took from the experience a unique understanding and appreciation of the dynamics of change. I was absolutely on one side but it was almost as if by accident and I could just as well been on the other side. Kids my age were in Southeast Asia killing and being killed, and I was in Chicago doing the same. I looked into those young faces and saw myself. While I was used to seeing the scum of the earth doing what scum do best and reacting accordingly, this was different. These were, mostly, smart middle to upper class kids who for whatever reason really believed in something and who did not reflect the party line or that of their folks. They were acting out on what they viewed as right and wrong and in so doing set the United States on a new course. That this happened in Mayor Daley's city, on my watch and on TV made it all the more poetic.

That convention is unique in our history. Where

else can a convention and all that happened around it be covered by the simple words "Chicago '68." We all now know about 911, but nothing changed the course of our nation as did "Chicago '68." This also marked the beginning of the slow decline and eventual end of the Daley Machine and its hold over the city. You know what they say about evil things (Bats, monsters, things of the night), keep them away from religious symbols but most of all, they must keep out of the light. Once light is shed on them they lose their mystical powers, as did Mayor Daley. It was hardly the end of the Machine or the Mayor, but some of the mystical aura was dispelled and change would come to Chicago in time. The emperor has no clothes, the emperor has no clothes.

Of course we didn't know the future implications for our city and the nation in that hot week in Chicago, but learned it much later. For us, the men in Blue, it was the varsity game, homecoming and the Super Bowl all in one. We had a hell of a time and got overtime to boot. Oh yes, almost forgot, I also got married. What a summer!

THE BEAST
AND
THE
BEAUTY

Chapter 20

I know what you are going to say, I got it back-wards, but this story is about dysfunction. We all live our lives in parts and each part has its own merit. As I write this I will say for those interested that today, many years after the time covered between these covers, I am happily married to Avemaria, my second wife. My first wife, Bonita died in 1999.

So back to the story. By any definition you wish to employ, I was a beast. I was short tempered, violent, harsh, dishonest, outwardly unfeeling and otherwise not such a nice guy. Except for the dishonest part , I have probably described the larger portion of single career cops everywhere. The problem is that if you are submerged in the lowest and most crass cesspool of life day in and day out you either drown, blow your brains out (in police jargon "eat your gun") or you erect defenses. The most typical defense is to develop a shell that separates you from the filth, but some stink will always stick. I said I worked hard, played hard, spent money with abandon and enjoyed life to the extreme. My motto was if I were to die tomorrow I would damn sure have a good time today. That was my world.

You know how I met my wife, but why she ever gave me a second glance is beyond me. The first glance was guaranteed as I was about to belt her with my baton at the riots, but believe me when I say that is the only time for the rest of our life together that I was ever even remotely tempted to strike her. She was that special!

She was small, beautiful and an intellectual giant. We came from the same neighborhood and she had street smarts, but unlike me, she decided to improve things whenever she could. She achieved several degrees, was a psychologist, High School Counselor and respected civic member of the community. She worked in soup kitchens for the homeless and did whatever it took to take the edge off the harsh world she saw around her.

To this day, I cannot tell you or understand myself why she took an interest in me. We were night and day, polar opposites, as different as different gets. If there is one saving grace in my existence it's that I married her and that we had our beautiful children. I was following a quick path to destruction, physically and mentally. I had been shot, stabbed and beaten and had given back in kind. I was at times dishonest (Part-time, but still a serious hobby, and all I knew was Law Enforcement and the dark side of life. That I was Jewish in an Irish and Italian world just hardened me all the more. I was always walking the line and at any moment could fall off and it would all be over. The kicker was that I loved my life and would never have changed. To change any destructive behavior, drinking, over eating, spending, you first must want to change—and I didn't. In all likelihood, I would have ended up dead or in jail; for me it was in for an inch, in for a mile.

By getting married and having kids, all of a sudden everything changed. Bonita was that rarest of women who could encourage, end an argument with one word, reinforce and also not ask what she knew I could not tell. She let me be me and at the same time, allowed me to become so much more. I was never a civic reconstruction project for her; there was just this attraction that opposites experience and together we made each other whole. In the latter years of my police career, I found I lived two distinctly separate lives, my life on the streets and my life with my wife and family.

Bonita achieved great acclaim and prosperity in her chosen field and was socially well connected. She would often be invited to exclusive dinners and events (The type you read about in the papers the next day). As her husband I was also included. She would admonish me not to embarrass her in such company and I did the best I could, but most times found a way to trip up. This was as much by purpose as by accident and became almost part of the show. There she would be talking theory to someone and I would be standing by the bar. Someone would invariable come up and ask if I were her husband and what I did. I always answered truthfully. I was so out of character with all around me that I became a minor celebrity in my own right and was always asked what police work was like. Maybe I was an oddity on display, but I never tried to intentionally embarrass her before her friends and peers.

She was small and I large. I could break her

in half in an instant, and she could always wrap me around her little finger—just how it was. I changed, and perhaps again that's one reason for this book. When she was alive, she urged me to write my story down, that it had merit, but we never quite got around to it. I'm sure she was proud of me and felt there were worthwhile lessons to be learned. Time and events have a way of sidelining or derailing good ideas and this was no different, but if my ranting in these pages has an ounce of decency and value, you can thank her for that—as I do.

The particulars of what eventually happened are not all that important, but even then there were meaningful lessons to be learned. Bonita had and eventually passed from cancer. For five years, she had level 4 cancer and yet kept living and working, far surpassing the projections and expectations of the experts. Not once did I ever hear her ask "Why me," or complain about her misfortune. While all around her were crumbling, she was planning and directing.

It's an obvious fact that we all are born to eventually die and in a sense the fact that she knew what she would die from and approximately when instilled in her a type of freedom she thrived on. While her body wasted away, her mind reached new levels. She was the strongest person I have ever met and handled the question of her mortality with, and this from a Jewish boy, saintly grace. She planned her funeral and was absolute that all in the family continue with their lives, and she provided good direction for each to follow.

When she did die, there were two-page spreads in both major Chicago newspapers telling of her accomplishments and how much she would be missed, but they themselves missed her greatest accomplishment, me. She turned me from a brute and a monster to something so much better. She allowed me to look at myself in both a critical and compassionate manner and to decide finally, after 20 years, to leave the department and find a life in the outside world. Yet she never despoiled or marginalized my time as a cop. As a good friend has said to me, we are the sum of our parts, so how can you disparage a life choice made years before if it is part of who you are today?

All I can really say is thank God I almost clubbed that little girl during the '68 Democratic Convention. They said-and still say-that Convention changed America and her path forever. Little do they know what else that week did, that it changed my life.

Chapter 21

I was teamed with a great man, a great cop whose name was Jack Marcus. This was an unusual pairing since he was also Jewish, though that had little to do with anything. Jack and I, Starsky and Hutch, two buds with their own style that complimented. At this time we also had a good relationship with our Supervisor, so this was a good time to be a cop.

One day we were on routine patrol in our unmarked car when a call came in: "See the woman at some address on obscene phone call." This sounds pretty garden variety, but nothing else was doing so we responded that we were on the way. Perhaps 15 minutes later, we arrive at a neat five-story apartment house; upper scale. We knock and she has us come in. She explains that she has been getting obscene phone calls regularly from the same man and they are escalating in vulgarity. For some reason this perv thinks he has something going with the young, attractive woman and wants to meet for a date. While we are getting this down, this fucker calls and she picks up the phone and talks to him. We write on a slip of paper "Have him come to the Mom and Pop Market two blocks down in three hours and you will see him." He agrees!

We wire the young lady and tell her to get him to say something incriminating and we would get it on tape and arrest him., But DON'T GET IN HIS CAR, we cautioned her! We are there with the area staked out at the appointed time but first 15 minutes pass, then half an hour, 45 minutes, and he is a no show. We call the show off and send the other support units on their way and Jack goes into the store to get a couple coffees when I see this nice car pull up by our young woman. I try to motion Jack to get back in a hurry but he is intent on looking at some skin mag and was not paying attention. Talk about asleep at the wheel. Then our girl goes to the passenger window and talks to our guy, which I get on tape. The door opens and she gets in. The car pulls away from the curb and I honk for Jack and he comes running. We call in 2060 engaged in a chase, possible kidnapping and sexual assault in progress. Anytime you call in an "In progress," the gloves come off. With siren on, we are now in a high speed chase (The Hutch would have been proud) and after eight or more blocks we come up on some heavier traffic and he is penned in. We rush the car, one on each side with guns drawn, pull open both doors at the same moment and yank him out the driver's side and our girl out the passenger side. We were none too gentle, with him for being a pervert and her for being so fucking damn dumb, even for a natural blond. We precede to beat the living crap out of the suspect and only stop when it is apparent we have an audience and that we might actually kill him. He was well dressed, maybe 6'3" and 185 pounds. His glasses are twisted and shattered, nose, ear and lip bleeding and he seems in shock; probably the first time in his life he was on the receiving end of a whooping since recess.

We haul his sorry ass into the station and book him. Turns out he has no record, is a grad student from a local university in Urban Planning and is from a very good, well regarded family. I hear later that he copped a plea and, since it was a first offense and non violent, he was released with a minor slap on the wrist.

Sgt. Jack McCalley and I are sitting at Bert's restaurant having breakfast several weeks later when a beat cop comes in and gives us a copy of the daily bulletin. The lead item concerned a report of a young woman beaten and raped in front of her child, knocked unconscious and the flat set on fire. She is in serious condition but did manage to say her attacker had made a lewd call to her prior to his breaking in and she described our guy to a T. The frosting on the cake was that her apartment was two blocks from our first girl's place and just down from the Mom and Pop Market. This could not be a coincidence. We arrange for a picture lineup, go to the hospital and see the victim. She is a terrible mess. She was disfigured in the attack and scarred in the fire, but nothing compared to the scars she had to live with in her mind and soul. Those scars would never heal.

She looks at the photos and when she comes to our guy she lets out a scream that could only be compared to a wild animal in its death agony. I have never heard anything like it, but it stays in my mind.

Jack, Sgt. McCalley and I return to our car and our anger could not be greater. We drive directly to the suspect's apartment and enter and go up to his door. His first name is Alvin (like in the Chipmunks and he looks just as intimidating). We stand on either side of his door and draw our guns. Jack leans over and knocks and we announce that we are the police and to open up. The door opens and there he meekly stands and he says, "Officer Cohen, I have been waiting for you." We don't have a warrant with us so we ask Alvin if we can come in and he says yes. We walk inside, having holstered our pieces and what we see freezes us in place. Large black garbage bags fill the room to a height of several feet with passageways weaving through to the various rooms, each of which also are stuffed with garbage bags. If this fuck planned to try and get off with an insanity plea, he was doing a pretty darn good job of it.

Turns out our meek little Alvin was a serial rapist whose crimes were escalating in seriousness, but he was already up to attempted murder and arson so he was about to graduate. His family ties might still help him, but he was going away for a very long time, either to prison or a mental hospital. Unfortunately, his victim had a life sentence.

This is one of the few times in my career that I seriously wished to be judge, jury and executioner, but to my shame, better sense prevailed.

Oh yes, you are probably wondering what happened to our little Chipmunk; he walked. Lest we forget this is Chicago and we had (have) the best justice money can buy.

Chapter 22

Sometimes a good idea goes very wrong and, with 20/20 hindsight, it should have been obvious.

The idea was to offer a free concert in the park. Summers are always a problem in the inner city-hot, sticky and nothing much to do. You notice there are few riots in the winter when the chill wind off the lake is 20 below and you need to tramp through the snow. Trouble is mainly a summer pastime.

So here we are, the end of a very hot and humid day and all have come to see Sly and the Family Stone perform, a free show. The crowd consists of hippies and blacks. Next ingredient to be added is the police presence. The elite of the force, contrary to conventional thought and wisdom, are the traffic cops, all of whom wore white hats. As mentioned before, being a traffic cop was a grealy sought after and prized position for its obvious lucrative opportunities.

There were perhaps 9,000 people in the park. Many were drinking and smoking (Not tobacco). I was assigned to assist in crowd control along with another guy or two from our downtown location. In all, we totaled around 12 officers for the entire event. The day was growing long and still no band and the natives were starting to stir. We were getting uneasy so we clustered together and put our backs to the band shell. Now the natives were restless.

Finally, word came that there would be no Sly and the Family Stone (I guess just missing in action), and the announcement was made. There was an unnatural silence followed by a low rumble and grumble. It sounded like the earth was going to shoot forward with fire and brimstone. The crowd slowly started to stand and move to the front. "Looks like we may get a real stampede," one of our older cops observed, and this just two years to the day of the '68 Convention.

We continue to back up until we were touching the stage and then we all climbed up on stage and stood shoulder to shoulder. The crowd, many of whom had been drinking for hours, was getting very loud and angry. Things were being thrown and the mass of humanity started to move toward the Clam Shell. As far as we were concerned they could have the damn stage. but we were backed into a corner and had nowhere to go. This was starting to look a lot like the Alamo and, as with the Alamo, there were no chances for reinforcements. The streets leading into Grant Park were all in solid gridlock so no one was going anywhere.

The hoard was continuing its advance and here and there you could hear screams and gunfire. We turned to the senior officer present, a traffic Sergeant and asked what he thought we should do. "I don't know about you guys," he said, and he took out his revolver and fired six times into or over the crowd. We then did the same. There is no telling who, if anyone we hit, but the crowd did stop and went the other way. It was them or us and we decided it would not be us, not that day. Obviously people were hit, but if by us or other concert goers it was impossible to tell. The crowd did stop their advance and moved from the Park into the streets of Downtown Chicago, causing destruction along the way.

There was surprisingly little reporting on the incident in the papers or on the news. No accurate accounting of how many were shot or injured was ever released, though it was a fact that there was shooting from the crowd at the crowd during much of the exchange. Personally, I don't think anyone really wanted to wade into this pool at that time so it was left to die its unnatural death. This does, however, illustrate a point and that is: when backs are literally against the wall, cops will stick together much as brothers anywhere. No way was anyone going to erect a statue to the fallen 12 (Or however many of us there were); we simple chose that it would be the other guy.

As an interesting side note, Barack Obama held his acceptance speech as President Elect of the United States of America in the same Grant Park, and not that far from where this incident took place. How the world has changed. I thought to myself what a difference 40 years or so can make in the life of a people and a country.

But for us that day in 1970, the sweet music was our footsteps in walking out of the park when all was over.

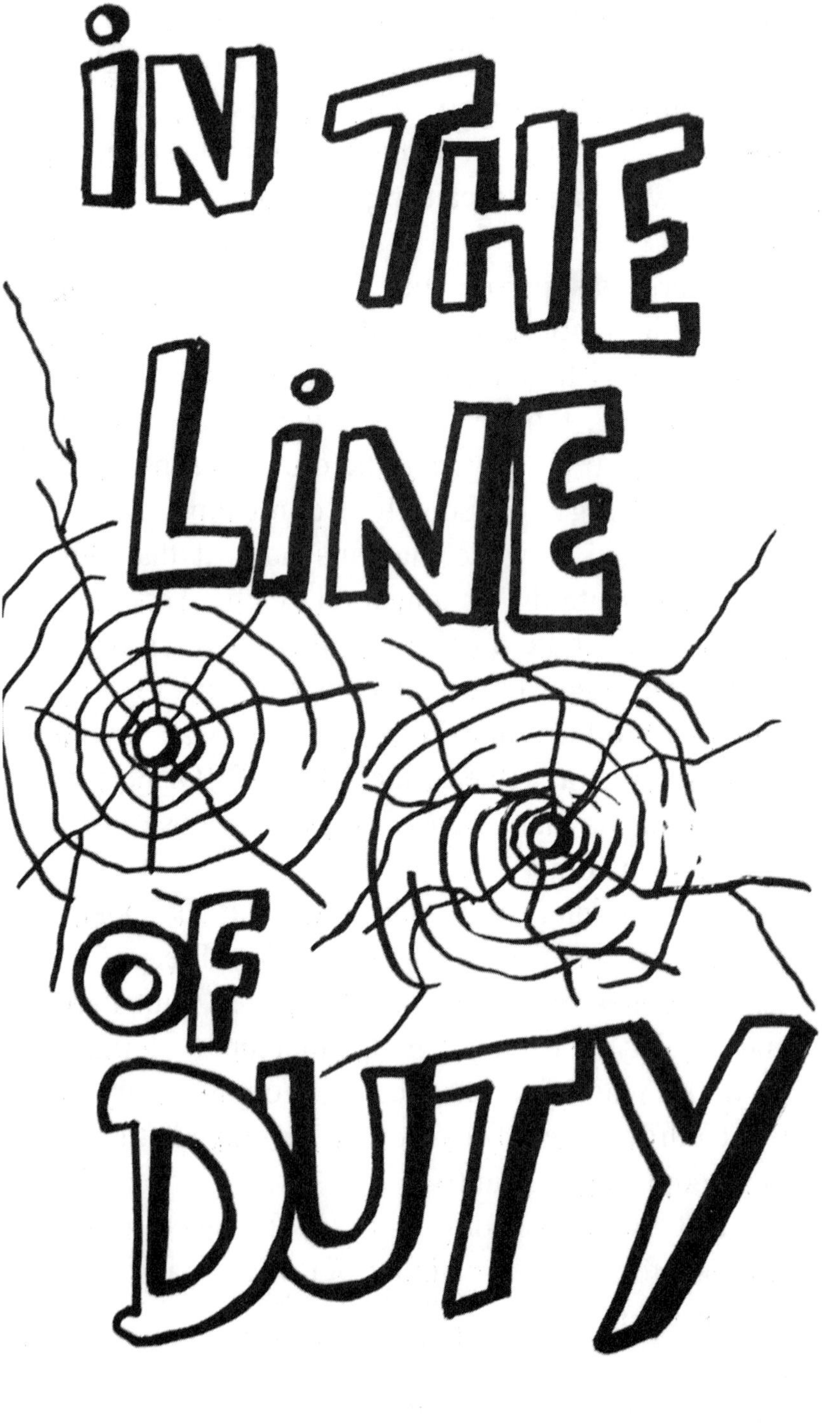
IN THE LINE OF DUTY

Chapter 23

I make a big thing out of the dishonesty angle of being a Chicago cop and that is one of the main areas of focus for this book, but I don't want it to detract from the good police work that took place and the many fine officers who did it.

It's fun to talk about the sensational and to shock and tantalize, but for the vast majority of the 20 years I spent on the force, the work done day-to-day was in service to the people of the city of Chicago. We were not hoods driving police vehicles looking constantly for scores, but rather rough-hewn, rugged individuals doing a job that paid poorly and looking for the perks that the position offered. We didn't invent the system and it existed after I and my friends left, so it was what it was.

On a daily basis, we would strap on our weapons, adjust our hats, polish our shoes, have our coffee, read the paper and gather with others of our kind for eight hours of patrol and observation. It's much as they describe being in combat in the army- 95% boredom punctuated with 5% terror.

No matter what their specific transgression, should a cop fall in the line of duty, in my book he goes down as a good cop giving his all for his community. I never knew anyone in law enforcement that was all one thing or another, people are complicated, lives are complicated, situations are complicated and how we live our lives is, well, complicated. We were not punched out of dough with a cookie cutter, and in the 60s and 70s there was more the old school and tradition than new school, technology and propriety. We were taught to knock heads, take names and be the wall that separates the good citizens from the denizens, and I believe we did this job well. We were probably not the refined individuals you would wish to ask over for dinner on Friday or Saturday night, but we were the ones you would pray for when threatened or victimized. We did work for ourselves, but mainly we worked for you and did not lose sight of that commitment.

Were we more brutal to the crooks and felons than we had to be? Sure. Were we willing to take as well as receive? Certainly. We all occupied the mean streets and played by street rules; to do anything else would be suicide. As Chcago changed, as the country and the world changed, so did we. Women came into the department, technology arrived and codification established that removed guessing and replaced impulse with procedure, but at its essence we were the thin line that allowed good people to live their lives in relative security and enjoy the fruits of their labor.

Even those few cops who had Mob affiliation would stand up and do their duty to serve and protect if and when the situation dictated. Something about putting on the uniform, of the brotherhood of like individuals and shared adversity that knits a department together. By most any standard, those of us who worked the streets in those years can be criticized or worse for actions taken but we took our duty seriously and day in and day out showed up and hit the streets intent on putting our lives on the line for our city.

Anyway, that's my take on those years.

I've talked about the inmates running the asylum, and that is true. If shit rises to the surface, then you knew where the supervisors came from in the Department.

If you were Irish, you might go somewhere in the Department. If you were "Connected" or part of the Mob, you probably would rise in the Department. This is not something you just learned, you knew it going in, so no sour grapes. Understand that Chicago has a long history of lawlessness, but also a long history of strong rule from the Mayor's office. Most everything was a scam, and if you peeled away all the layers of the onion you would run out of onion before you ran out of crooks in government. That said, there existed another dichotomy: the cops loved their city with a passion.

One day at roll call, before the night shift, I was daydreaming when the Captain came in with a request. Peterson Avenue parallels the main runways at Chicago O'Hare Airport. It seemed so many officers were making traffic stops along that road that the concern was raised that approaching aircraft may confuse the Avenue for the runway and land in the wrong place. Chicago Police cars have blue lights that are very similar to airport lights.

If you were transported to Chicago, the city

might look familiar. *Hill Street Blues*, the cop show, was modeled after the area around the Academy and that is also where the *Blues Brothers* was filmed.

So is Chicago that different from New York City or perhaps Compton or Rampart District in California or any major city for that matter? The answer would be yes and no. All major cities and their Police Departments have problems, and these problems are cyclical, with disgrace interspaced with reform and good intentions. However, in Chicago the culture is more entrenched and the corruption more widespread. I would have said that this was true in the 60s and perhaps this was unique to that era, but similar concerns are being raised at this moment in Chicago (Though that is beyond the purview of this story or my personal experience).

I would only say that if it looks like a duck, swims like a duck and farts underwater like a duck, well then we are probably looking at a duck, or in this case the Chicago Police Department.

Chapter 24

Late in my career, around three years prior to leaving the force, I was assigned to a new station in an upscale neighborhood. You know how it works when there is a new anything, such as expansion football teams; each existing team must send a couple of players to the new club to get them started. Obviously, you never send your good guys, so this is seen as a golden opportunity to get rid of the dead wood (me).

I had my usual hear-to-heart with the new Captain, some youngster out of daycare, and after I threatened to kick his ass and he threatened to have me taken outside and shot, we reached some accommodation and life went on.

The new station was pathetically understaffed and then not with Chicago's best, so on the graveyard shift, starting at midnight, we typically had four guys driving desks and only three on the road. With this staffing, we each drove one man patrols.

I received a call while driving my beat, "See the man." Turned out the man was night security at one of those ritzy, swank, and overpriced apartment complexes. I pulled up and went in to talk to the dude and he says a big, really big man and a little chick came in and disappeared. "Disappeared," I said, "Like in Houdini disappeared?" "No, I just don't know where they are, but they definitely don't belong here." "I am thinking, I don't belong here either." "Do you have a laundry room?" "Yes we do." "Is it equipped with pay washers and dryers?" "Yes again." "And where is this laundry room?" "Right over there."

Off I went to the aforementioned laundry room. There had been a rash of thefts from similar laundry rooms in the past couple weeks so this was starting to look familiar. When I get there, I stand by the door for a moment and listen, and much to my surprise I hear sound from within, and it isn't swish, swish, swish. I was dressed for the miserable winter weather outside and had on a heavy jacket, sweater and all the rest. I pushed open the door and here is the big, really big guy kissing the little chick. "Okay, break it up," I said. As they were untangling I took a look around the room and noticed two things: the walls and floor were heavy white tile and the coin boxes of the various machines had been jimmied.

As I turn my attention once more to the big, I know, really big guy, I see he is coming my way and before I can react in any way he stabs me in the upper right chest with a long industrial screwdriver, the same one I surmised he had just used to relieve the pay machines of their collected change. The screwdriver digs into my chest, but with all the winter clothes, only slightly penetrates my body. I instinctively pull my weapon, this time a .45 super and am about to plug the fucker when reason intrudes on my plans. It is obvious that if I shoot him with such a high velocity round, it would bounce around the room like a mad ping-pong ball and we would all probably end up being shot.

I reholster my piece and dive into the guy and we become a tangle. He was, as I said, big, really big, but I am good sized also, so it was a real knock down drag out. He gets the upper hand, but I quickly follow with an upper cut that takes him down for a moment. Out of the corner of my eye, I see the girl start to move around, trying to get behind me, but I look over and say, "If you move I will shoot you in your fucking face," so she backes off. The guy starts to get the better of me, but slips up (Actually slips), and I use my strength and diminished judo skills to throw him feet first into an open large dryer, the type with a glass window in the front. Somewhere in my mind I envisioned closing the door and putting in a couple of quarters, but he is so big he won't fit all the way in. He tries to get out and I keep slamming his head with the dryer door. The facility guard, while all this was going on, had called 911 and said, "One of your officers is getting killed," and provided the needed information. When no one from my District responded, units from adjoining Districts start to show up. The first cop rushes in to see me smashing this dude's head with the dryer door and tried to pull me off him, so I cold cock him and he goes down for the count and I continue to smash the fucking suspect with the door. Other cops and cooler heads then show and the fun and games come to an end. And I was having such a good time. This could have looked bad for me except that the security guard had watched the whole thing unfold on his security monitor and the first thing he says is, "I have never seen such restraint on the part of a cop before. If it were me I would have shot the guy."

So far so good, but with me, so good only goes so far.

The TV news and papers report the incident fairly accurately, but then go on to criticize my District for its lack of response and general unprofessional behavior; now I'm screwed but that's hardly new. Nobody was happy, but at least I eventually skated.

Turns out the MF (Motherfucker) who attacked me was released just days before from the Pen and was just too busy to get a real job. I next saw him a few weeks later when he was brought before a judge. The really big guy also had a really big mouth and attitude to go with it, and manages to really piss off the judge. The judge was so mad he decreed the trial would start later that afternoon and within a day this guy was back in the Pen.

So the moral of the story is: "Don't step on my cape." Don't piss off the judge and go to jail, directly to jail, Do not pass go and do not collect $200.

Another action packed day in the Windy City.

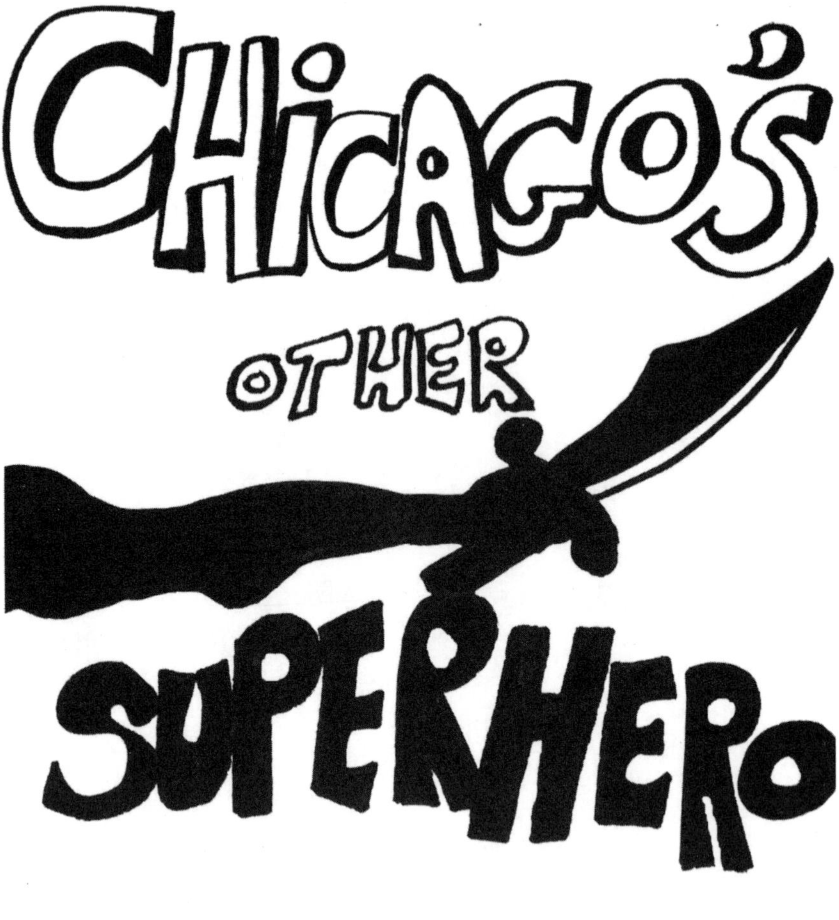
CHICAGO'S
OTHER
SUPERHERO

Chapter 25

I knew, worked with and was a friend of Sergio Oliva from 1981 to 1983.

This name may mean nothing to you, but don't ever let Sergio hear you say that. Some people are so unique and famous that they are known by only one name, and Sergio is the Myth, the original, the one and only.

Sergio defected from Cuba where he was on the Olympic Weight Lifting Team. He eventually found his way to the Windy City and became a police officer. Oh, by the way, he was also Mr. Olympia '67, '68 and '69 and eventually lost to an upstart, a Mr. Arnold Schwarzenegger

Sergio was a genetic freak, and after him they didn't have to break the mold, he broke it just being born. Steroids were legal and a part of the equation in the 60s and all competitive body builders used them. In Sergio's case they only enhanced what God had already given him. Sergio was Chicago's original Super Hero, both in reputation, and some would say, in fact. And he was my partner for a time.

He was no cartoon creation and was, in reality, a force to be reckoned with, the real deal. I will describe him in the event you are still not familiar with him, but I guarantee you would stop and stare if you were to meet him on the streets.

Sergio was black, had a shaven head the size of a bowling ball, weighed over 240 pounds of solid muscle, with a 28 inch waist. Each leg came in greater that that measurement. His uniforms were custom made, of course, and he was instantly recognizable by one and all, and no, he didn't wear a cape. He was, again obviously, fantastically muscled in a defined way and was a force of nature to be respected.

When partnered with him, it was not business as usual, but more of a promotional tour. He could break up fights just by taking off his coat and saying hello. A typical day would begin with our leaving the station and stopping by the local donut establishment; Sergio would order two dozen of their best and from there we would go on to breakfast. Breakfast consisted of perhaps a dozen eggs, pound of bacon, loaf of bread and a gallon of milk, and this would hold him until lunch. He had the metabolism of a hummingbird in the body of a mighty California condor (largest bird in the United States). I am a good-sized guy, but next to him I looked like the proverbial 90-pound-weakling.

On the plus side, working with Sergio, confrontations were few and far between, but there are always the few who don't recognize the Super Heroes, or are just too stupid, and that's when the fun began.

We went on one call, between dinner and whatever that meal is between dinner and breakfast, to a Syrian social cub. It seems while socializing, a fight broke out between 15 or 20 good friends and they were well into their fun as we arrived. We were the first car on the scene and proceeded in to the club only to duck flying chairs, fists and dinnerware. Sergio, as is his custom, stood majestically and surveyed the scene. In most cases, that was all it took and the participants would cease their activities to say hello and perhaps get an autograph, but not here. I don't know if these guys were new to America or the planet for that matter, but somehow they didn't know royalty when they saw it. I was standing behind Sergio for my protection and in case, well, just for my protection. Sergio was getting really pissed that he was not getting the acknowledgment and attention that is due a man of his stature and accomplishment. He proceeds to take off his winter jacket and is now standing there in his custom fitted blue police uniform. This should be enough to stop even the gods of Olympus in Greece, but again his magnificence was just not working that evening. This was simply too much to bear and the mountain that was Sergio took umbrage. I knew the real fun was about to begin.

Sergio waded into the fur ball and, one by one, as if in a cartoon, bodies started to fly through the air in all directions. After the first 10 or 15 combatants had collected in various piles around the room, the remaining party-goers saw the error in their ways and decided this was one Police Officer they had better honor. During the brawl, I received a call from Dispatch asking if we needed backup or assistance. I responded by saying Sergio, ah we, had matters well under control, but that they may wish to dispatch several ambulances, a couple wagons and maybe the garbage collection folks to our location as they are sure to be needed.

You may wonder how it was that Sergio and I became friends and then partners. I frequented Chicago Health Clubs, one of the first gyms, and Sergio also went there. On arriving in Chicago, he first went to the Duncan Y, which was a mecca for body builders in the Midwest, and later he switched to the Chicago Health Club. We would work out with weights and in conditioning and after a while, he became aware of my reputation, my interest in the martial arts and marathon running. He helped me with the weights and I helped him with, ah, well something or other. We just kind of clicked, but I didn't patronize him and truly liked him and I believe that was appreciated.

Sergio stayed on the force even longer than I did, always as a patrolman. He had his choice of jobs but elected to stay in daily contact with his constituents and I believe the feeling was mutual as he was larger than life and a visual reminder of the dedication required of a cop and their love for their city.

In another situation, we were called to the Elevated Platform. It seems a disturbance on a train was in progress with a very drunk and belligerent rider harassing the other passengers. We arrived and walk up two flights of stairs to the platform where the train, now stopped and screwing up the entire system, was sitting. The conductor advised us of the situation and Sergio goes in. With me backing up the big guy, as usual, we enter the train and are confronted by this very large, very drunk and very obnoxious individual. He slurs out, "What you guys want and what you think your gunna do bout it?" Sergio isn't big on conversation and he just steps forward and picks up this fuck and holds him over his head like a rag doll. By now the other passengers recognize their Super Hero and they are clapping, cheering and talking to Sergio. All the time the mope is kicking and swinging his arms about, but is pushed up against the ceiling like so much trash. After a nice question and answer session, we decide it's time to return to our patrol car. Sergio simply walks out with this drunken slob over his head and carries him down the two flights of stairs and throws him into the back of the squad car.

Sergio, again in true superhuman, superhero fashion, had not even ruffled his custom tailored shirt. He suggests that on the way back to the station we stop off at the all night donut shop and get a dozen or so to go. So went that night and many like it.

I will say that no one's life is easy or without problems and Sergio was no exception, but he was always a heck of a friend and a partner you could depend on. Those several years were a highlight for me and provided comic relief to an otherwise gritty existence on the mean streets. He was an original, and I have always wished Sergio well and trust he is enjoying his life to this day.

Chapter 26

We've already seen examples of what one human life is worth, and sometimes that value is nothing. The single greatest cause of violent conflict then, as now, is perceived disrespect. Case in point.

In the 20th District, you find the great contrast of people and lifestyles. In one extreme, on the north side you have a predominately Jewish neighborhood of considerable wealth and prestige called West Rogers Park. Crime in this well patrolled area is mainly burglary. The crooks are the aristocrats of crime, the professionals, and the skilled practitioners of that ancient art. These guys never packed weapons and knew when to give it up; you could almost respect them.

In the sharpest contrast imaginable is the south end. This is the destination of American Indians and Appalachian peoples who migrated from the back woods or hillbilly areas of Kentucky and other states, to seek some sort of employment in Chicago. These people, are displaced populations within their own ghettos. Most cops hated to go into these areas and when they did, it was always in numbers. I can't say which is worse, but I can give you a few examples.

We received a call about a knifing in an Appalachian shit kicker bar. I arrived with a few other officers and immediately see a man sitting on the front wooden steps, holding his intestines. If that were not bad enough his heart, still warm, is sitting next to him; obviously he was beyond caring. Since this is not something you see every day (Once a week maybe, but not every day), we were a bit transfixed. Suddenly a man comes out the front door with a bloody, dripping knife in his hand and surrenders. I talk to him, and this is how the conversation went. "Ah, hey guy, why did you gut and cut the heart out of this fellow here?" "Cuz I from West Virginia and he sid he wos from Kentucky and he disrespect West Virginia, so I showed him a lessin. Ain't no one can sey thet bout West Virginia, nohows." I responded, "Guess he won't make that mistake again." In both ghettos, hillbillies and Indians, guns are never used, it's always knives.

Another time we get a call from Dispatch to go to the home of one of these guys and slap the cuffs on him and bring him in. My partner and I get to his house and we go up to his front door. We knock and the door opens... behind a screen this small, raggedy attired woman, is standing "Ah, is Johnny Fuck Face here?" "No sers, ain't herez." "Do you know where we may find him?" "He went to the Bucket of Blood." "Ah, do you know when he is expected back?" "Said hee'd be home after he beets the fuckin' sheet out of sum cops, so'z meybe in a few ours." We thanked her for her kindness and left, figuring we didn't need to arrest him and next week would be fine. No cop or two cops could walk into one of these bars and get out alive, so discretion was the better part of valor that week and Johnny could just enjoy himself a little longer. One last thing about these guys: most came from the coal mines of West Virginia and Kentucky and were skinny, stick figures but who were also the strongest, most powerful people we ever saw, almost impossible to cuff.

We received a domestic disturbance call and responded. When we got to the residence, we went up the stairs and knocked. A lady answered the door.; She was messed up, her hair all over the place, dress torn and an oozing purple black eye. "We had a call of a disturbance from one of your neighbors and wanted to check and be sure all was Okay." "Evrythin's fine." "Doesn't look fine to me," I responded. At this moment the wife's husband comes up to the door and he is a piece of work-drunk, wearing only an old, sweat stained T-shirt with droopy shorts. "Can we come in?" I ask. He nods and we go inside. The living room had furniture overturned, a small fish tank on the carpet with a couple gold fish still flopping now and then. "Doesn't look fine to us, Sir. "Did he hit you?" we ask the wife. Tears come to her eyes and she nods slightly. "Since we didn't witness the assault we can only take him to jail for the evening." "Jahil!" they both say, "ain't goin to no Jahil," he says. Then he makes a fist and slugs his wife hard, right in the face and she goes down like a lead balloon. "We cuff him and say, "Why the hell you do that? Now we have to arrest you and you'll be in for some time." He answers, "If I can't heit my own wife then I wants to be in jail." As we turn to leave, the wife jumps to her feet and onto my back and starts swinging her fists, hitting my head and shoulders. For this we arrest her also. It's not at all uncommon in situations such as this that when the husband, the familiy's only source of support must go away, the women react violently. That's why most cops will tell you they hate domestic violence calls.

I will say this about the shit kickers; they are standup guys. What I mean is that you will see a guy with half an ear missing and a badly broken nose and ask what happened. He will laugh and say a cop beat the fucking shit out of him the previous night. They have a certain dignity that accepts the damage from fights as a badge of courage. Their women, typically attractive when they arrive in Chicago, turn into people with broken noses and missing teeth, and they scar up almost as quickly as their male counterparts. These people just love to drink and fight.

The Indians were twice as bad, and that describes the good ones. Indian bars in the area had names like Reservation, Big Mikes—and lest we forget, the War Bonnet. It is no exaggeration that Indians cannot hold their liquor. If you go into an Indian bar you WILL, absolutely, positively, without question be stabbed. They got me with a blade in the butt once. It is pure suicide to enter such an establishment. Indian women are almost twice as violent as the males and will as soon castrate you with the flick of the blade as look at you.

Whether Appalachians or Indians, this ritual bloodletting and cop fighting is considered simply good fun and something to be enjoyed. Since there were knifings in both communities most nights, we didn't try very hard to sort things out. Our rational was that while they wouldn't talk to the police, they also wouldn't complain about us and they stayed in their own areas. They just had these little worlds and as long as they lived (And died) in their ghetto and didn't bother the rest of us, they could castrate, gut, collect ears, scalps or whatever to their hearts' content, unless their heart was sitting on the stoop next to them (Public health concern).

Chapter 27

I'll tell you right now, don't read this chapter right before or after a meal; you've been duly warned. There has to be someone to do the dirty work and in Chicago up until recently it was the Paddy Wagon crew. The Wagon was a utility vehicle for most everything. You need to move prisoners or detainees, call the Wagon. You need to move a body from the hospital or morgue to the funeral home, call the Wagon. Dead people in auto accidents or home explosions, murders, natural causes, dead Martians, call the Wagon (For the last entry, also call NASA and a tabloid). Floaters, Wagon. Drunks, Wagon. Dead animals, Wagon. Hookers, Wagon. Vagrants, Wagon. What I really hated the most were the "Crispy-critters", those who died in fires. They smelled terrible, were crunchy on the outside and gooey on the inside, and they made funny faces at you.

My partner for most of my Wagon "career" was Officer Waldimer (Wally) Shreck. Wally and I were referred to as the "Bruise Brothers."

I had transferred from 24th District (Rogers Park) to the 23rd District (Town Hall). The Commander of the 23rd was a Nazi (sympathizer or for real), and I had a long history with him. He decided that he would screw me over royally and partner me with another German, Wally, but he didn't do his homework. Wally was a young malcontent. After four years on the job, he was burning out and needed alcohol and drugs to get by. Wally was one of the strongest men I have ever met and true enough, he was all German (but he was actually Croatian, so that's how fucked up this was), but more of a German Shepherd than Waffen SS. Wally was a sweet, simple man doing the wrong job for his temperament, but was as loyal and protective as a fine Police Dog (And I mean absolutely no disrespect in any way to Wally). We shared many experiences and he saved my Jewish bacon on several occasions.

We did hundreds and hundreds of calls, but here is one very typical one for your edification.

Dispatch :Squadrol 2372

2372 Responding

Dispatch 2372, There is a strong odor coming from the fifth floor at 39- Kenmore

2372, 10-4

Upon arriving at 39- Kenmore, we were greeted by the Building Manager and advised there had been complaints of rotting garbage from an apartment on the fifth floor, Apt. 501, and he didn't want to go in without us along. By now we knew what the problem was, but why spoil the surprise? We get to 501 and I ask the Manager to use his key to open the door. I tell him to go in first and that we would follow. The key goes in, the manager goes in, the manager comes out and vomits all over the floor. "Must be a lot of trash in that place," I say and Wally adds, "Must be." Obviously, the now "Late" renter of Apt 501 has been dead for several days. Mr. Apt. 501 does not look human anymore, but is now a Sci Fi creature that is black and green, a bloated mass that is twice the size of a person and looks like it is ready to pop and thousands of little aliens will scurry forth, maggots calling him home sweet home. You call your Sergeant and he comes over, glances in and says after a quick peek, "Natural causes. Get me the report and transport the man from the Gooey Nebula to the morgue." He makes a quick retreat. You call the coroner and he says, "Fine, transport him (is it a him?). "We think so." We get a Ziegler Box from a local funeral Home. This box is a metal coffin and a screw top for gooey guys like our fellow. We bag him in a really thick body bag, zip him up and make sure all the parts are in there. We then screw down the top. You have your partner, when he goes for the box, to also get some Vic's Vapor Rub, some Formaldehyde and two cigars. The Formaldehyde is for the gooey stiff, the Vapor Rub goes up your nose and the cigars just seemed like a good idea. You are on the fifth floor and of course the three of us (One in a large metal box) won't fit in the elevator so it's five up and now five down. We don't want to drop our new client and hurt him, so we are pretty careful. Before we leave the apartment, however, we have as much time as we please to really throw the place and see what is there. As stinky a situation as this seems, its really heaven sent and potentially very lucrative. I guarantee you are never disturbed.

There have been rumors, the type old men tell

around a camp fire under the stars while passing ...a bottle, the tale of the team that found the suitcase stash under the bed, filled with loot. Other tales of riches and treasures unimaginable, but for Wally and me no such luck. Sure, we got some fine knick knacks, booze, and some bucks for the weekend, but no treasures. If a natural death you need a death certificate, but if the guy had seen his Doc in the past 30 days, that would do. You then took the semi liquid filled box to the Funeral home, get your pay-off from them for your bringing them the business (Usually $10-30) and then it's on to the next call.

The messy ones often came from the Marine Unit. A floater would be found and the Unit would retrieve the body, but we would do the transport. If the floater had been in the water for some time the Officer on the scene would usually have a rookie pull it out of the water. What the Officer knew and the rookie would find out is that often as not the arm came off like a cooked chicken wing and the rest was still floating.

Lest I forget, there also was the blue light special. On late evenings, we would pick up drunks off the street or DUIs and have to transport them. Some people are funny drunks, some are sleepy drunks, some happy and some just mean and nasty. Since I am large, we were usually called to get the mean and nasty. I had to force or encourage them into the back of the truck and sometimes they fought back. Now I never lost such a fight nor was I going to give anyone the satisfaction of having to report that a prisoner almost got the best of us. Instead I just put them forcibly into the truck, left them handcuffed with their hands behind their backs, but didn't buckle them in. We then would take the long way in, maybe along Lakeshore Drive. We would hit 40 mph or more and slam on the brakes then whip the truck this way and that-just like an old Batman movie: "Bing, bop, bang, kabang, boom and back to bing." We then delivered our tenderized charge to either to the emergency room or to jail.

Oh yes, the blue light special: all police vehicles in Chicago have blue lights.

PLACES EVEN THE PADDY WAGON DARE NOT GO

Chapter 28

In 1985, I had about as much of police work as I could stomach, at least the action part, and you could say I was just burnt out. I found a way to be assigned to the Paddy Wagon and found life just a little more agreeable. Wally, who appeared to be somewhat slow and habitually drunk, stoned or both, was otherwise a good guy. His demeanor was camouflage for a pretty sharp guy with a bizarre sense of humor. I had a deal going with Wally: he shows up clean and sober and stays that way for the shift and I would do all in my power to make sure we did not work beyond that which could not be avoided. It was a Sunday and Wally announces that he is thinking seriously of moving to the N.W. side, which is about as far away from our station area as you can get, but for a Paddy Wagon, calls can come from most anywhere, so to the N.W. side we go. It takes two hours to get there and we know that shortly we must make our way back or be found tardy without a hall excuse.

We kick the wagon into high gear and lumber off, trying to swim upstream and get back while it's still light out.

This thing looks like that contraption in the movie *The War Wagon*, a big box on wheels with little openings. Traffic is getting bad and our situation is also worsening. We hear radio traffic and some calls along the lines of "Paddy Wagon, where are you?" Off to the right I see a turnoff that belongs to the Railroad and think I see a way to shave minutes, if not a hour, off of our journey. With traffic at a grid lock, my lights and siren would do no good on the bridge but the RR landing might work. I hit the lights and peel off, going down an incline and onto the RR tracks. No trains in sight and, if I am right, this will take us to the heart of our District. I drive on, supremely confident in my judgment and more than a little superior at my plan. Wally says, "Gary, isn't this the track the trains use?" "Well yes, Wally, but you will notice they are not using it right now and we are an official law enforcement vehicle." Then he says, "Hey, why are we so far off of the ground?" "Ah, shit, didn't see that coming." Seems the foundation for track which had been going down was now starting to go up and at a pretty steep angle. This is getting to feel a lot like the first big hill for the Mammoth Roller Coaster, and then we reach the top and it flattens out. Just below us is I94 (The Kennedy Expressway), the roadway we were on earlier, when the wheels freeze in place. Seems the track had elevated some from the bed and was just high enough that it caught our wheels and froze us in place.

This is really not turning out too well and I can just see the headlines, "Top Crime Fighter falls to death in Paddy Wagon from a train crash over I-94. Was it a Mob hit or simply stupidity?" You can make a good case for stupidity this time.

I tell Wally to get out and try to push the back of

the Wagon, but that is to no avail. The sun is starting to fade. Then I recall an Amtrak Special comes through three times per week, but is it M,W,F or T,T,S, and what of Sunday? I see four kids playing on the tracks some distance ahead and get out and yell to them but they run. I take off after them and get pretty close and say I am not a cop today, and will pay each kid $10 to help move our vehicle.

Together we break the wagon free and I back it down the hill and onto a flat surface by the bottom track; a half hour later the Amtrak Sunday Special thunders by.

As the sun sets over the city, you could often find Wally and me sitting in our Wagon, front wheels up to the breakwater at the furthest part of the land where the park ended and the harbor began, contemplating the evening in the Windy City and taking in the beauty of flashing blue lights winking along Lake Shore Drive. One such evening, we were relaxing in particularly deep contemplation, with Wally enjoying his favorite beverage as I was just smoking and starting to nod off. Suddenly there is this sharp rap on the window. I roll it down and it's an Inspector who states with pride and authority, "What the hell are you two doing out here, sleeping on duty and serving no police purpose?" "Not so, good Inspector," I intoned, "We are of Dahomey faith and you have just interrupted our evening prayers." "Please leave before our God places his wrath upon you, and don't make too much noise and further disrupt our devotions."

THE "GREATEST" OF THE GREAT LAKES

Chapter 29

Lake Michigan. The defining feature of Chicago is its location relative to the lake and the lake of note is Lake Michigan, one of the five Great Lakes. Lake Michigan is the only Great Lake that is within the borders of the U.S. and is the fifth largest lake in the world: 307 miles long, 118 miles wide with a shoreline of 1,640 long with an average depth of 280 feet. The deepest depth in the lake is approximately 925 feet. The lake is a year round highway for heavy commerce and the transport of steel, iron ore, grain and basic materials from state to state and through the locks with access to the Atlantic Ocean. The Lake is protected and maintained by the United States Coast Guard. The lake is Chicago. Lake Michigan is a deadly mistress and gives off a siren call. This because during the day in late spring or early summer the air temperature may be 90 degrees, but the water temperature can hover around 50 degrees at the surface. This is a deadly situation when combined with alcohol or the unwary.

Growing up I was born on the North West side of Chicago, but moved at age 7. My old neighborhood, while not Shangri-La, was, a very pleasant working class community comprised of Jews, Poles and an emerging Puerto Rican population. The homes were mainly one-family bungalows (Called the Chicago Bungalow), and there was harmony between the various ethnic groups. We moved just before the neighborhood's transition to a hotbed of Latino gang influence.

We relocated to the North side one block from Lake Michigan. I spent most of my free time at the lake front. During the summer, I could be found there from sunup to sundown at one of the many beaches that dotted the extensive shoreline. I went beach hopping. I would swim daily in the Lake, no matter the weather and came to know and love the Lake for the fine Mistress she is. There was a Nike Missile Site, which was an antiaircraft missile operation, and I would secretly fish for perch around its perimeter.

Dreams can come true The Lake had waves just like the ocean. In the winter, the waves would freeze over into giant ice floes with fantastic shapes and of immense size. To the trained eye they looked just like pirate ships of old under full sail. Boys my age were dreaming of becoming doctors, lawyers and Indian chiefs; I dreamed of being a pirate and I was one of the few to achieve my dream. Instead of a three mast brigantine, I took sail in the Blue Cruiser with a large engine and a siren that would still the soul, and I got to practice my dream. In the olden days, pirate ships would look like everyday clippers and haulers, but would pounce on their victims without warning and raise the Jolly Roger. There is nothing finer than to fantasize as a kid and then be able to play for real-and be paid for the play is even better. For me, Sheridan Road, which ran parallel to the lakefront, was akin to the Barbary Coast. I knew every cove, backwater and inlet, and I never took prisoners.

As a beat cop, I would often cruise Sheridan Road doing my preventive aggressive patrol, as instructed by police General Orders. We would frequently receive calls from the 30-story highrises that dotted the Lakefront and looked out over the water. Most of these calls came from the numerous residents who had their telescopes overlooking the Lake and these reports were of spotted submarine periscope masts or Great Lake monsters. The report of an occasional ship sinking would also come in. One day, however, a call came in of a swimmer holding on to a buoy approximately 200 yards off shore at Berwyn Avenue Beach. I responded and was met by a lifeguard from an adjoining beach. It turned out we knew each other from years past. He said, "Do you want to take a swim?" and I answered, "let's go." I stripped down to my skivvies and locked my uniform and equipment in the Squad Car and entered the water and its six foot waves. "Don't ask where I put the keys." We swam out to the buoy with some difficulty and found Omar clinging, too exhausted to make the return swim. We are treading water and getting smacked around and told Omar to jump in so we can make it back to shore. Omar turns out to be Omar the chicken shit. He just loves the buoy and is a no go. I waited for a wave crest, and on its rise smash Omar in the face and he dead ends into the water. The lifeguard and I grab him and drag his sorry ass back to shore. The good thing for me is that I got to go home early and, that I also received a commendation for saving a voter's life. My little adventure doesn't hold a candle, though, to the most heroic event I ever witnessed as a police officer.

The most heroic thing I ever witnessed, or no good deed goes unpunished. Several years later, while working the 23rd (Town Hall) District along the jogging path at Lincoln Park, I happened to come across another Squad Car with both front doors open. I come to a stop and exit my car and see two cops I know standing on the large breakwater concrete barriers. One of them is stripping down to his shorts and jumping into the water. This was late April and it was warm out, but the water had just recently melted from the ice flows and was hovering around 40 degrees. Ralph Culver (Ralfie) was swimming out to an overturned flat bottomed rowboat around 300 to 400 yards out. There were four heads bobbing on the surface. I told Ralph's partner to call in to the Fire Department for an emergency helicopter rescue as anyone with any brains would know Ralph couldn't get back to shore. I see him reaching the victims just as we hear the helicopter approach. It had been in the vicinity and airborne and diverted to our location. As Ralph approached the swimmers, two disappeared under the surface and were never seen again (Alive). He proceeded to the third and fourth person and held on to them while treading water. The copter didn't have a basket on board or emergency swimmer, but lowered a harness. It was designed for only one person. Ralph grabbed the harness and held one of the people with his arms and one with his legs, but halfway up the one held by his legs slipped and fell back to the water and drowned. The helicopter crew brought both him and the one survivor on board and rushed them to emergency at Northwestern Hospital. Both were treated for extreme exposure and had to stay for some time.

We visited Ralph the next day and commended him for his bravery. We said he would be the town's hero and was a shoe-in for promotion, meritoriously, which we pointed out was way better than posthumously. We also suggested he check with his doctor to see if the hospital did brain transplant operations since he obviously needed more brains. Sure enough, the papers declared Ralph a hero who prompted the then mayor of Chicago, Jane Byrne, to visit him with congratulations and the good news of a new assignment. She says with great pride that he is now being assigned to the Chicago's elite Marine Unit to which Ralph, who only wanted a promotion to Sergeant said, and I quote, "What the fuck, I hate the water," and that was that. The perfect end to a perfect story. I have to say this is the single greatest, most heroic act I have ever witnessed. Once more, it only goes to underscore what I already knew, no-good deed goes unpunished.

Chapter 30

Port of call Finger Dock Belmont Harbor, 25 foot sloop called Breezin. This was my sailboat and escape from active days policing and every now and then I and some of my buds would pick up a case or two of Buds, and set sail for a three-hour tour. These short trips would calm the savage soul and allow for a good unwind, and we always looked forward to our forays away from land. One evening, I set sail with two of my fellow cops and we headed out. Just beyond the breakwater, one of my intrepid travelers advises that we need to turn around and head back immediately. "Why?" I inquired. "Because I am getting seasick and need to go back now." "Well, it will take another hour to turn around and get back and it's too early for that, so no can do." Then I see out of the corner of my eye that we are approaching the large bell buoy used to navigate the entrance to the harbor. I say, "Tell you what, I'll leave you at this buoy and pick you up on the way back. Better yet, I'll leave a couple beers with you." I noticed that he had on his jacket and warm clothes so he'd be all right. Anyway, we leave him and continue on with the tour. A couple hours later and it's getting dark and we head back to shore. When we get to the harbor we remember that we forgot something and after considerable thought we recalled what it was. Did we lock the car when we set out? Just couldn't remember. Oh yes, our pal on the buoy. We were so very tired that even the thought of going out again would spoil an otherwise wonderful afternoon and early evening, so we called in to the Marine Unit and reported that we noticed a cop holding onto a buoy at the harbor's mouth. We said we thought he had been drinking, but could they pick him up at their convenience.

On another occasion, one of the good guys, the Sergeant who first got me on the force, will go down in history for one thing and one thing only: reporting that Lake Michigan was on fire.

He had been "Working" the late night shift and was considering the essence of the universe while parked by the lake on Lakeshore Drive (Asleep) when he was rudely awakened by old Sol himself, burning his way up over the horizon. Anyone who has witnessed the sun rising from the Lake knows what a dramatic thrill it can be. All at once it seems as if the entire horizon is consumed by the brilliant yellow and red orb that gets larger and brighter as it rises further into the morning sky. "Dispatch, Dispatch, emergency, Lake Michigan is on fire, it's on fire man," he shrills. "Ah, Okay, well we haven't heard anything at this end but once the sun is up we'll get a better picture of what's happening" Over the open mike comes only two words, "Holly Shit!" I am afraid Sarg was never able to live that one down, and after such a good night's sleep.

In Chicago the lake is the character and soul of the place and also the one thing that allowed Chicago to start when and where it did and still be of such great importance today. In most every way, the lake is to Chicago what the Atlantic Ocean is to New York and the Pacific is to Los Angeles. Our history is woven around the lake. Al Capone used to bring beer and rum down from Canada in fast speedboats called "cigar boats" or by large trucks in convoys. That was Prohibition. Then was then and now was now, but the city that works, the 24-hour city that allowed for Big Al Capone and Frank Nitti, also allows for the vice today. Chicago is a city of destination; there is only one Chicago. Anything you want or desire can be had there, from the finest haute cuisine to authentic Irish or Italian dishes. If the story I am telling took place in, lets say, Racine Wisconsin, I doubt it would be of any real interest to readers, but the fact that this happened in one of the most famous and storied cities in the world makes it newsworthy. I may be talking about yesterday and the day before that, but understand please that some things just don't change or age well, so I am "Probably" talking about today and tomorrow as well.

Back to the Lake. Late in the day as the sun sets, you will usually find several police vehicles parked by the shore. We have a saying, "When the sun goes down the rats come out." The biggest rats you have ever seen live in or around the breakwater rocks. These fucking rats are so big they can talk. They've been heard to say in a low voice, "Here kitty, kitty, kitty."

So the rats would come out and we, the cops, would take out our .45's, .38's and 12 Gauge shotguns and blast away. Ricochets all over, whining sounds, twangs, and the sparks on the rocks; you just would have to be there to appreciate it. After a while, the shooting would die down and Dispatch would call and put a concerned citizen on. "Sir, may I be of some assistance?" I intone. "I hear terrible amounts of gunfire down by the lake and need to alert the police." "Have no fear, good Citizen of Chicago, your alert has already been noted and we are at the location even as we speak."

LAW AND DISORDER

Chapter 31

Remember that nagging little child's game you or your sister or your neighbor played? You just wanted to smack them. You just described not only the Chicago Police Department but most of law enforcement and intelligence nationwide. It's not "I'll show you mine if you'll show me yours" it's more "It's mine and you can't have it, you can't have it, you can't make me."

Any Police Department is set up much as a medieval community with all manner of smaller fiefdoms and dukedoms, which in turn are made up of clans, societies and secret societies. The point is that everyone has his or her territory to protect-their perceived acreage and all other boundaries, natural and contrived. Dogs and wolves have these also, except rather than putting down stones to mark boundaries, it is done by peeing on posts, trees and other landmarks in the area, thus telling others about the ownership of said area.

In most any police organization you have Vice, Burglary, Homicide, Car Theft, Robbery, Narcotics and the like. Each of these is a small fiefdom, and as with any good fort, the defenses are formidable. You take serious umbrage with anyone from any other area that infringes on that which is yours and that only refers to the sharing of intelligence. If successes are had by outsiders, they are stealing your thunder, shaming you and rubbing your nose

213

in it. To say that cooperation between different departments in a police organization is non existent is a serious understatement; there is actually open warfare.

Taken a step higher, no Police Department welcomes interference by the FBI or other state, local or national organization. All play it close to the vest lest someone else takes credit. This is nothing new and, in fact it, existed on 9/11 and perhaps to this very day. You might almost forget that we are all working for pretty much the same thing.

In the 60s, this problem was so ignored that it wasn't even viewed as a problem, more as just the natural order, the way of things.

I was assigned to a "Crime car" that was later to become a "Tactical unit." The street cops had their own streets to patrol, traffic their corners or stretches of city streets, and the Detectives had assigned cases and a case load. Of the bunch it was only my group that had what may be viewed as a portfolio at large-the mandate to investigate anything anywhere (In their assigned district) with little oversight. We were by design freelancers or nomads who were expected to have a particularly good nose for crime and plenty of street smarts. Our "team" consisted of a Lieutenant, a Sergeant and perhaps eight other officers. Of our eight street guys, most had their specialty (Guns, burglary, robbery, etc.). We supported each other as required and were the tip of the spear regarding serious crime in each district.

In some ways, we were like those commandos

or marauders used in the South Pacific during the Second World War. We were used essentially behind enemy lines, hit and run, small, fast units with heavy firepower and a mandate to disrupt or stop illegal activity where ever we found it. I know, we need look no further than our own ranks, but that takes a blind eye to what we felt we were really obligated to do and that is to fight serious crime. On several occasions, I would have coffee with people whom I knew were players or burglars. We would discuss the "What if's," the "Suppose." We didn't really trade arrest for information. It was rather "You do me a favor and I'll do you one." In a strange sort of a way, this was neutral ground and a way to share concerns and look at the bigger issues. Several times after such a meeting, the Burglary dicks or another such unit would corner me an hour after the coffee and demand to know what I was doing with their suspect, their informant, or at least what was I doing in their backyard. As was my custom, I said nothing. few liked us; we were either meddling in their affairs or were busy setting things up for ourselves and cutting them out. No matter how you sliced it, we were seldom welcome. We inevitably stole their reputations, or their thunder, and we were roundly hated for peeing on their fence posts. To the entire world we looked like the glory boys, reporters' pets, out of control and dangerous, very romantic. For ourselves, we didn't give a fuck; we were doing our job, a very dangerous job, and doing it our way. We were often in the papers, on TV, and news reporters knew us by name and the like. With each exploit our stature and reputation grew until we were the talk of the town. Generally, this type of notoriety is frowned upon as being a God complex.

We felt we were fighting a war and had to muster all that we could find to be sure the fight was one-sided and decidedly not fair. Only fools play fair, and though we were at time less than honest, few people have ever suggested we were fools. To do so would have been, well, foolish.

There is another old saying that there is honor among thieves. This, I have found, is true, at least until it becomes inconvenient. Then it's each man for himself. I have come to the understanding that you can't change the past and it's wrong to try or to reconstruct it, but if you can learn from your experience and put that knowledge to some good use, then all was not negative or lost and something worthwhile can come from it. The error is to ignore, or worse yet, to deny the past and one's part in it. This is the ultimate dishonesty because you are lying to yourself and hoping you and all others believe it.

There is not a cop show on the air worth its salt that does not solve its assigned crime or misdemeanor in the hour allotted. Actually it's more like 38 minutes as the rest of the time is dedicated to commercials. We accept this for two reasons: 1) commercials are what pay for the programming, and 2) these cops make the streets safe for all of us. So this is reaffirming.

This is as far from the real world as you can get. Nothing in honest to goodness police work is tidy or timely. Your gun is heavy and awkward, you typically don't wear your seat belt because you need to move quickly and not get tangled up. When you call Dispatch, they often know nothing more than you do about something. Thus, you are always making educated guesses or judgments on things. TV cops have those witty sardonic lines, the sneer, wisecrack, great timing, awesome driving ability and almost perfect crime solving skills. When have you ever seen one of these folks trip over a loose shoe lace, do a header trying to get out of their vehicle or call their partner by the wrong name? In their running gun fights with shots being fired all over, ever see a dog fall over dead a block away or someone's planter turned into dust? How about those fantastic automatic weapons they use, the Uzis and submachine guns that not only never run out of ammo, but don't discharge brass all over the area. Ever see a cop be burned by grabbing the hot barrel of a just-fired gun or running out of bullets and throwing their firearm? How about piss breaks or maybe they just don't do that sort of thing.

Reality has it that most crimes are never solved and, for many, there is not even an attempt to do so. The usual suspects may be an entire neighborhood, and there are some places the cops just won't go. In the real world, a cop has a sense which car to stop because something isn't quite right. Racial profiling, of course. If you are black or Hispanic you are going to be in for a bad time—that's just the way it is. If you are white middle class and look the part, you probably won't be harassed.

What isn't widely acknowledged is that the police are structured to respond after, that's "After" a crime has been committed, not before or during. If the crime has yet to happen, there is little if anything the cops can do for you. If you go about your business blindly thinking law enforcement will protect you and look out for your welfare, you are sadly out of touch with reality.

I have solved crimes within minutes of their happening, days later and for the most part, never. The only factor that brings me any sense of closure is that crooks and malcontents are almost always repeat offenders and sooner or later they will trip up. They may not be tried for their most egregious action, but eventually they will pay a price. If the crime is high visibility or against a child, the prison system and fellow prisoners help take justice into their own hands and the results aren't nice—crimes against kids are not well received.

Crooks tend not to be the brightest bulbs on the tree. They generally enjoy drinking, doing drugs, bragging and spouting their mouths off. They simply need to hear themselves talk. As corny as it sounds, the old technique of good cop bad cop works most of the time, but the answers come from listening. An old mobster I once knew said to me that all the real bad guys are either dead or in jail. That is the end of the road practically for someone who spends his life in pursuit of easy rewards.

Law enforcement in reality is a scattered, report intensive, rule abiding process that has little to do with catching thieves and much to do with political correctness and CYA. This is not a tidy process and not at all like television; I like to call real world policing "Law and Disorder."

MY DARKEST

CHICAGO
POLICE
DEPT.

TIME

Chapter 32

Y ou are probably expecting me to talk more about my wife and her untimely death, but I view that to this day as more of a life reinforcing experience and an example of heroism. We all die, but she accomplished so much and was the least traumatized of all involved by accepting it with grace and dignity.

No, my darkest moment came on the job and is still etched indelibly on my mind and seared into my consciousness. Some things are just so horrific that they never totally leaves you, remaining just under the surface.

I was working the Foster Ave. District when I responded to a citywide call: Police shot at a tavern located a few blocks from my location. When such a call comes in, all else is put on the shelf and all available units respond; these are brothers and they have been shot. I was one of the first to arrive. I drew my weapon and cautiously entered the bar. It was bright outside and dark within, but I had been wearing dark sunglasses and took them off so my eyes had less transition time than usual. As the gray, indistinct image clears, I see two Chicago uniformed Special Operations officers lying on the ground, almost touching, in a common lake of blood. I also note that both of their weapons are missing. I quickly ascertain the shooter has left so I tend to my brothers. Other officers are now in the bar and a flash message is sent identifying the assailant with a description. Instantly, I put in a call for emergency medical and ambulances, but know instinctively that both are gone: too much blood, way too much blood. They are transported within minutes but are declared DOA at Edgewater Hospital. As they were put in the ambulance for transport they are covered with white cloth and I have this terrible image of seeing the bottoms of their feet sticking out, red with blood and grime, the blue of their trousers and those white cloths covering them. I see the red bleeding through the white cloth and spreading out in a wider and wider circle, almost a living thing as it happens. Tears come to my eyes, hot tears. Here are two of my brothers, brothers in life and now brothers in death. This is the first time, I had this experience and it hurt terribly. It turns out to be the smallest of things you remember, and in this case it was the contrast of their blue pants and the red of the blood, and the understanding this could have been me.

There were many witnesses to the shooting, including patrons and the bartender. It seems our guys, Bruce Garrison, Star number 14775 and William Marsek, Star number 14086, got a lead about a jewelry robber who would be at the bar. Our Special Ops officers are the best trained, most professional, and it was incomprehensible that two could be taken down that quickly by a nobody, a fucking nobody.

The killer's name was Cohen (no relation), but we found this out later. At that time we were working from an alias. The killer fled to Milwaukee Wisconsin. A special team of Detectives from Chicago went after him, cornered him and killed him. This is the only way it could go down.

I attended the wake and funeral of the two fallen heroes. Both officers were resplendent in their finest uniforms and every cop not otherwise on critical duty was in attendance. I could not help but notice the stares of people who read my name tag. I quickly looked away. I was never so ashamed of my last name.

BOSSES-
SOMEONE
TOLD ME
TO TELL
YOU

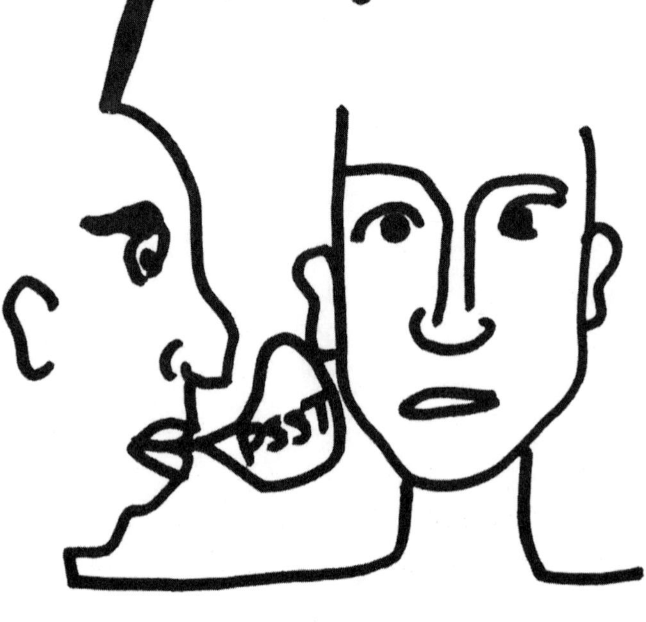

Chapter 33

The Boss is the leader of the pack, the chief honcho, the top banana, His Honor, the one and the only, Mayor for life, Richard J. Daley. The buck stops at his desk and the orders like little raindrops descend from the heavens on the heads and shoulders of lesser men.

One man a dynasty does not make; it takes several and it takes a plan. We spoke of the "Machine," but not of how this works day in and day out in all things Chicago. Mayor Daley's friend from childhood was Frank Quinn, Fire Chief Frank Quinn to me and you. To be clear, Mayor Daley loved the Fire Department. What's not to love? These are brave men, tried and true and everyone loved them. The Police Department was an organization no one loved, a necessary evil; the city needed order and Mayor Daley needed his army. Someone needed to keep the lid on the ghettos while the good men at the Fire Department put out the flames on the Gold Coast and elsewhere. You knew the Fire Department was better than the Police Department because it cost about $250 more in 1966 dollars to buy your way into the former vs. the latter.

It's all about image, and that has little to do with reality. Chicago is a happening town and you don't want convention attendees to have to worry about little things like crime, so there was none. How's that, you may ask? Simple. Crime statistics are kept by all major cities and supplied to the FBI for inclusion into the National Database, or NCIC (National Crime Index Center). Progress or the lack thereof is measured by watching if the little bouncing ball is going up or down. For the good Mayor, you control crime by controlling the statistics. A homicide can "reasonably" be shown to be a natural death, rape can be assault, or perhaps battery, and burglary becomes theft. As the song says, "You say tomato, I say tomahto." The first District has very little crime. The FBI thought this was just a little too good to be true, and true it wasn't. Actually, to properly quote the FBI, their word to describe this phenomena was "bullshit."

This was worrisome to the good Mayor, but a petty thief called Richard Morrisey or the Babbling Burglar, was an even bigger embarrassment. Our Mr. Morrisey was caught red-handed and in good order spilled the beans. Among the beans were several police officers, and this outlandish story turned out to be true. This was just too much—to be blind-sided by a burglar. Mayor Daley was pissed as his political future was on line so things were going to change, lad, things were going to change. For the first time in Chicago history an outsider, Mr. Orlando Wilson of California, was brought in and tasked to help select the next Superintendent of Police. After extensive interviews and research he had to advise Mayor Daley that no candidate was found within the Chicago Police Department who was qualified for the position. Mayor Daley then asked Mr. Wilson if he would accept the position and Chicago now had a new Superintendent of Police. Mr. Orlando W. Wilson, a criminologist and theoretical sociologist, had zero, nada and no practical experience as a cop. When theory meets reality, the results are not always pretty and this is pretty much what happened.

Wilson quickly initiated several programs that ran counter to the grain of Chicago's finest. He established open testing for the first time. As a result newcomers to the Department were now qualified personnel as opposed to political appointees and buy-ins. He abolished most two-man cars and substituted one man patrols. The idea was that two men together could plan and carry out crime, or worse, they could waste time talking and bull shitting, but a single cop could not. Then he completely decentralized the whole Department. A key element of the Chicago system is that once rank is awarded (even to the rank of Captain), and it can never be taken away. This often leads to a large number of bumbling underachievers who you keep for life. With this system, the old guys stayed but the new guys were now intellectuals and not of the mold— and they stayed also. Civil Service cuts both ways.

To understand Chicago and all that is written in this book, you need to understand how rank works. All rank positions from Patrolman to Captain are Civil Service. The exempt ranks made up of Commanders to Directors to Deputies were appointed at the pleasure of the Superintendent of Police or the Mayor. The importance of this is that an exempt rank of, say, District Commander could be held by the Civil Service rank of Lieutenant and still have three Captains working for him. Because of this he has to be careful that the people working for him today could be his boss tomorrow. These are appointed jobs so experience has little or nothing to do with anything. After six years of Superintendent Wilson, things that were bad were now worse. So he was sent packing, along with most of his fucked-up ideas.

Immediately the Department undid what Superintendent Wilson put in place. There was a return to centralized management and political appointments and the new police era was over (RIP); business as usual was once more at hand. Now, as God and Mayor Daley had intended, appointments were made with the help of political connections, the Mob, the Church or buy-in, and it all came down to clout.

Clout—such a simple little word, but oh so very important. "The China Man" was the man with clout and clout was the pure essence of everything. It was who you knew, what you knew and who you had in your corner, your clout. Favors were collected, bought, parceled out and hoarded ready to use on that rainy day or in furthering one's career.

I think an example might help here. When I worked the Superman Caper, our group was broken up and our commander replaced by another. My new Boss was Terrible Tommy Cernan, and he was an old fashioned in-your-face salt. He was on his new assignment when the call came in for me to report to his office. We hadn't met, but in both cases our reputations preceded us. This guy took no shit and was known as one tough customer by the rank and file. I went in and he looked up and said, "I know about you, yeh, I know about you." I answered, "I don't see any future for me here in Mass Transit working under you as I assume you are bringing in your own guys." "Good lad, you see things correctly, so what do you want?" "Rather like to return to the 20th, where I started." "You got it, now get out and tell the next clown to come in." That's just how he was, but that's okay by me. Turns out a few months later he gets bumped upstairs and is now the District Commander and his kingdom now includes the 20th. Small world! It didn't take me long to fuck up back at the 20th. They had this Captain who for some reason years earlier had died. He was gone for around two minutes, but he returned to the world of the living. However he left part of his brain on the dark side, and was easy to bait. He would always respond to requests or challenges by saying, "Go pound salt up your ass." Nobody ever figured out what that meant.

The problem was that, as a Captain, he had to work around the clock. I was assigned to protect the head of one of Chicago's larger parks as he had received threats from a gang. His hours were 9 a.m. to 5 p.m. so my hours were now 9 to 5. The Captian didn't like that I was working such a prime shift. One day, I get to the station at 4:45 and prepare to check out. The Captain spies me and says, "Hey, you there, Cohen, where you think you're goin?" "Home." "Like hell you are, get your ass back to the fuckin' park." "Captain, my shift is over in 15 minutes so if I go back to the park I won't make it in time and I will need to put in for OT, so I need an OT authorization from you first." "In my office, you, NOW." In to his office we go. I purposely leave the door ajar. He says, "You get your fuckin ass back to that park and I mean now." "No, I won't," is my answer. "What the fuck you mean by no, you little shit!" This is funny since I am 6'2" and he's 5'6" (maybe) and he is calling me a little shit. "Go fuck yourself," I say. "I'll break your balls, you little toad." "I can't hear you, can you say that a little louder?" "I WILL BREAK YOUR FUCKIN' BALLS, YOU SHIT." "WHAT YOU SAY?" "I'LL KILL YOU, YOU FUCKIN' SHIT, YOU'RE DEAD, YOU'RE DEAD, YOU HEAR ME?" and he starts to chase me around his desk. We do a couple of orbits and then I push the door open and out we go. By now the entire floor is still and watching this little fucker chase me in circles around the squad room and screaming, "YOU'RE DEAD MOTHERFUCKER, YOU'RE DEAD. POUND SALT, YOU FUCKER, GO POUND SALT UP YOUR ASS!"

Finally the Commander comes in and sends the Captain back to his office and then asks me, "What the hell happened, Cohen?" And I honestly answer, "Got me, he just went nuts and started chasing me around his desk. Scared the shit out of me, he was just insane." "Okay, I'll take care of this, but do me a favor and just stay away from him for a couple days and let this calm down."

Score one for me, but tomorrow is a new day and it's back to work. I report to my guy at the park around 9:00 a.m. and he says maybe I'd enjoy a little basketball. The park is near the Chicago Bulls' practice facility. So it's the park guy, me, the center for the Bulls, Dave Corzine (all 6'11"), and somebody else, a forward who likes to fly through the air with the greatest of ease and do that fancy show offy stuff. I just can't quite remember his name, but he was pretty famous." So we have this 2 on 2 for an hour. After kicking some real tall butt, I decided to go easy on the guys and let them win. Then it's off to the showers and a nice round of golf. We tee off and my ball hits, but bounces off at an angle and ends up next to the chain-link fence just off the parking lot. We walk up for our next shot and I survey my lie. I have a golf jacket over my uniform and am surveying the shot when I hear a voice that says, "What the fuck you doing here Cohen?" It's the Captain and Commander Cernan. I don't even look up but said, "Trying to fix this slice I have, probably have to lower my grip some and choke up on the club." The Captain screams, "WHAT!" "I'm sorry, thought I explained that, seems I have this slice on my drives and I hope to fix the problem by moving my hands up and shortening my swing." The Commander, just standing there, says, "Makes sense to me." I take my shot and walk off leaving them both at the fence. This was just too, too much. The Captain puts in a complaint against me and places several charges with their corresponding CR's (Complaint register). Next day, I report to work and am told to go see the District Commander about a serious beef I am having with my Captain. I get to his office and Terrible Tommy says "Come in. Hey, Cohen, what the fuck you up to now?" I sit down and say "Don't know, Boss, Captain Robinson has just been going nuts and keeps chasing me and spying on me." He says, "Well, what are we going to do, he wants your hide on the wall. Got to give him something, he wants you canned, so what do you think?" "Well, I actually agree, you've got to quiet the old guy down, so maybe a written reprimand or something like that?" "Yeh, that sounds good, a written reprimand." Just then the door swings open and in comes Robinson. Before a word is said the Captain says, "I want this mudderfucker fired, I want him for insubordination, I want his ass for unprofessional behavior, I want his balls for being out of uniform. He is the worst, the most disrespectful fucker I have ever known and I want him off the force and I want it NOW!" Terrible Tommy says, "Captain, I've looked into all this and I am going to give him a very strongly worded reprimand and it will go into his folder." "Okay, that's done, so you have anything more for me?" Robinson can't even talk at this point so Cernan says, "Guess we're done here. Thanks for your information." The only thing Robinson can utter under his breath and which he keeps repeating as he exits is "Go pound salt up your ass, go pound salt up your ass, go pound salt up your ass."

The written reprimand never made it to my file. The moral of this particular story was that the Captain did not do his homework and did not know I personally knew Terrible Tommy and that I had clout. Better believe, word made it around the District.

This is a dangerous game to play since the source of your clout can die or retire and any number of other things can happen that change the dynamic. Also, I had made an enemy for life in the Captain, but then, just like that little brightly colored frog, he considered me as nothing before and now he has to wonder just how dangerous I really am. Never hurts to keep them off balance.

Its a funny world, the brass and the lower class. The guys stuck in the middle are the Sergeants, just like in the army. In the army it's the Sergeant Major, in the Navy the Chief Petty Officer. These are the highest enlisted ranks and they are the reason anything gets done. The rank and file follow their directions while the officers mainly never leave their offices and, in any case, rarely know what the hell to do anyway.

Sometimes, just like in medieval times, one sergeant calls out another sergeant from another watch. This is how one such incident unfolded. Sergeant McGreggor goes up to Sergeant Macklin and challenges him to a duel in the schoolyard at 5:00

a.m. the next morning to resolve ongoing disputes and perceived disrespect. At the appointed hour, McGreggor is there but Macklin is a no show. The next day, McGreggor goes to the station looking for Macklin, walks up behind him and without a word being spoken, Cold Cocks him right in the face and down he goes. The Captain of that particular watch, a political appointee, knows better than to become involved and closes his office door; "I saw nothing, I saw nothing." That settles the dispute and then it was business as usual.

Before and during the '68 convention, the rank and file and the Sergeants wore the same color uniforms-blue. There were no white shirts seen that day which proves there were no officers beyond a few Lieutenants who showed up; all others were holed up in their offices. After the convention it was mandated Sergeants now wear white so there could be some visual identification of command.

There are many other stories about my run-ins with authority, but the vast majority of officers in the Chicago Police Department were old, worn out and very poorly suited for whatever job they had. This trickled down to all levels and became the rotted core of the old tree.

Almost forgot, there is one last duty the Sergeant had to perform. When the message came down from on high, it was the Sergeant who had to meet with the one receiving such a message, intoning "Someone told me to tell you." So now you have been told.

SECOND PLACE IS FIRST PLACE

2nd Place

LOOSER

Chapter 34

We've all heard the "Second place is first place loser" expression this was never more true than in police work. There are two types of career cops: There are street cops who work for a living and put their lives on the line and there are the paper pushers who take pride in the fact that they have never drawn their weapon in anger. Obviously, the office type can go forever, give nice speeches and look great on TV, but it's the pukes on the street who define where the rubber meets the road.

General Patton (During the Second World War), was know as "Old Blood and Guts, " or as his men would say, "our blood, his guts." Wait a week and another initiative will come out of headquarters or City Hall and off we go chasing our tails again. Every time the shit hits the fan, the knee jerk reaction is to add more rules and oversight, by the paper pushers, to "Ensure that never happens again." It is literally impossible to be a street cop and conform to all the rules, or to even know all the rules, for that matter. This is known to one and all, the result being that if any level of leadership (I use the word loosely) wants to fuck you, all they have to do is take Volumes 1-37 off the shelves and leaf through the pages until they find something you're in "Flagrant or willful" violation of. Unless you know where the skeletons are hidden in the closet or have really well placed friends, you don't stand a snowball's chance.

There are other ways "The man" can shit on you. One of the favorite is for Commanders to communicate when you change Districts. Upon arriving, you are scheduled for the most unpopular assignments and shifts. Just when it's time for your day(s) off, you are sent on temporary duty to another District and work on your days off. Funny thing, when it's time for your days off, it's musical shifts again, and again and again. Pretty soon you burn out, fuck up or come in line. Gary, don't play that game. *

The best defense is a fucking good offense and I have been told I am a very "Offensive" person. The idea is taken from nature. Some fish, frogs and snakes don't blend into the background, but are brilliantly colored with distinctive markings. These adornments say to one and all, "Bite me and you die." It's just that simple. If your reputation is that you are always just slightly under control, though that control can vanish in an instant, then you are well marked.

I have been insulted by the best. I have been sternly advised that I could be replaced by a lower order primate and they could save money by paying the other monkey peanuts. I was a threat to management due to my close ties to reporters, both print and TV. I had my supporters, but the older the renegade bull gets, the more isolated he also becomes. After a time, I hadn't the energy or the zest for the

*This was prior to the F.O.P. police union. (Fraternal order of police.)

good old locking of horns and was more apt to leave that to the younger bucks. Being foolish and disrespectful is hard work and is a younger man's game. The closer I got to my magic 20 and the more outside interests I developed, the less I enjoyed the sparring.

This time in a cop's life is precarious and fraught with danger from all sides. You are still potentially up against the young thugs on the street to whom reputation means nothing, respect means nothing. I sought less confrontational endeavors such as the Paddy Wagon and enjoyed the company of like-minded people. I spent less time being physical and combative and more time thinking: I was, in fact, a very good investigator and solved many crimes through brains rather than brawn. My extracurricular activities scaled back appreciably and I began to take a critical look at policing, at the Chicago PD and at myself. In all cases, I was less than pleased with what I saw and knew that I would not continue far beyond my 20th anniversary. By that time, I had a wife and kids and interests well beyond cracking skulls. All were supportive of any decision I would make. In my view, the department, for all its half hearted reform attempts and reorganization, was still at its heart and core rotten and diseased and beyond repair. I didn't know what the future held for the Department, but I was certain they would arrive at their future destination without yours truly and that they would be every bit as dysfunctional and segmented as when I left. Some things by their very nature don't change. The reformers had come and gone, investigations both state and national were conducted, scores of cops were arrested. If they had wanted, they would have taken the entire Department down. That we got the job done at all is a testament to the reality that you are never all good or all bad. When called on, love of the city and respect for the uniform will ensure that the individual cop rises to the occasion.

Saving the citizens of Chicago is a young man's game, however, so I saw the writing on the wall. My days of frivolity were drawing to a close and I must leave my playground for more mature endeavors.

Through luck and providence I've seen trends come and go. I have witnessed firsthand the allure and temptation, the siren call of street officers. I have experienced the arrival of technology and seen the evolution, for good and bad, that has taken place to bring us to today's police "Culture" throughout the country.

If anyone doesn't wish to indulge my observations on this subject due to my checkered history, I would say 1) I understand, 2) who cares and 3) not to know history is to be condemned to repeat it.

Police work used to be an art, certainly not a science. You relied on your instinct, street smarts, physical advantage, and strength of character along with smoke and mirrors to achieve desired results and to remain alive (another desired result). We were taught from day one to be hard-nosed, forceful people who could take care of ourselves and the job and still produce results. We had little line management and the rule of the day was always "We want and expect you to get the job done and are not particularly interested in knowing how you do it." Police work was results-driven and we used all tools available; this included snitches and paid informants. We often had to sink to the level of the scum we were after to achieve results, and that was of necessity a filthy, degrading process.

Police work has evolved from around 1966 to the present and the difference is night and day.

So if you ask why should you listen to an old warhorse like me, versed in tools and techniques not used in decades and of questionable character? I can't come up with a single good reason other than that you might just learn something. In this book I honestly relate my strengths and weaknesses, my arrogance and simplicity, my fears and my sardonic humor to cope with those fears. I have seen way too much in my life and to my never ending unease, find I can live quite well with these images and the knowledge still fresh in my mind. I am not a stereotype of anyone and never tried to be what anyone expected me to be. But then I also never disparaged or found fault with my personal decision to enter police work and in how I conducted myself since. I worked to no higher calling than my own prurient interests.I always slept, and still sleep very well at night, thank you. So back to what I may offer and the only thing that comes to mind is that I have been there and done that. To kill in the line of duty is not an exercise in right or wrong, good or bad, belief or non-belief. It just is. I never received psychological help or analysis, never became a falling down drunken shell of myself or thirsted for more of the same. Again, thats just the way it was. I would say if pushed that I am pleased it's the other guy who's dead and not me. To say otherwise would certify that I am a nut job, and for sure you shouldn't be concerned with anything I have to say.

I spoke of the old days as the era of rugged individualism, characters right out of central casting and a thirst and hunger for all things. In the new era of police work, the pendulum has swung full cycle and now its cookie cutter cops, mind your manners, obey the law in all things, read them their rights. Its always Sir or Ma'am, forensics as the new religion, DNA as the great totem to truth and electronic instant everything. This stuff is great—wow. I wish we had some of it back when, but then we did get the job done with shoe leather, guts and teamwork; we were not pretty to look at but we were respected. Today, just like our cars, all cops look the same. Reliance on technology is so absolute that the art of the investigation, going with the gut feel, care of business has been lost. CODIS is a nationally shared database accessible by any agency or authorized organization, and can match DNA or fingerprints from most anyone ever entered in the system. Today cops are more autotrons plugged into mother, fed data from all places, the victims of information overload and psychoanalyzing everything to death.

The rule is point fingers, cross your T's and dot your I's and conform to the norm.

We have lost something fundamental in policing. While I do not suggest for an instant that we not pray at the altar of DNA, I do suggest that we spend more time developing our people skills, sharpening our minds and in a way hardening our hearts and skin when on duty. A cop today just as yesterday will need to find a coping mechanism, will need his or her support group, his or her cadre, will need to better use informants and other street resources and to keep a collective eye on the prize.

So if you are still indulging me (thank you), maybe you can see my theme here. Here is an illustrative example I just learned. The parachutes that are used on the Space Shuttle on the Solid Rocket Boosters are of the most modern materials available (Kevlar and Nylon), but the sewing machines used to fix the joints together and make the system space worth are a series of 1880 Singer Saddle Sewing Machines, well over 150 years old. The point is, if it worked and was a good idea then, it may well work and be a good idea now. Never, ever reject the advancements of science and technology, but use those gifts wisely and don't throw out the baby with the bathwater. Keep what you need and toss the rest. Use what you can use, but don't abuse. If you or anyone in law enforcement can find a balance between science and technology and the art of listening, thinking and acting proficiently, you will be the best cop you can be. That's all I am saying.

Had I at 22 started policing today, with my mind-set at the time I would have made a very poor cop. That I learned and survived over the years is actually the only career related thing that I take some considerable pride in. So if you would, please do as I say and not as I did.

I know you are dying to ask one question and since you are here in spirit only (or I am there in spirit only), let me pose the question on your mind and try to answer it. Question: "Were you ever influenced by the cop movies over the years and did you ever employ any of their signature moves in your real world work?" The answer is actually yes. I remember "Dirty Harry" saying all manner of neat lines such as "A good man knows his limitations" or "This is a .44 magnum and it can blow your head clean off," but in real life this became "Police, stop or I will shoot, NOW!" On the streets real dialogue is kept to a minimum. In the real world, if you are in a situation where your gun clears leather you don't announce what you are "planning" to do. You simply play by the rules and do it. If you take that shot, it is for body mass center not an arm or a leg, and two shots are always better than one. If you shoot it's with a deadly weapon and for deadly effect. By the way, the only rule that applies is don't give the fucker an even chance. The quicker you make your play or take the other out of contention, the quicker you can secure the scene and the less danger you and those around you find yourselves in. In the military today, the preferred approach to combat is to bring overwhelming resources to the conflict and to end it as quickly and as decisively as possible. The longer you are on the field, the longer really bad things can happen. Police work is no different. I would add one other thing: It might appear that I didn't employ during my career, is respect. You can show respect and still do the job and not lessen your authority. I have always found its better by far to have a one-on-one understanding than to burn bridges and lose a resource for all time. You may be a cop, he may be a crook, but you are both human beings and will react differently if treated with respect and firmness instead of disrespect and abuse. I can tell you there is often a very fine line between those who enforce the laws and those who break them. To think otherwise is to allow that all of life is black and white, when in fact it's shades of gray and blue.

There is only one other rule of the old road I adhered to and still feel is inviolate: If and when you start to question yourself, your motives and your ability, it is time to get out and find a more holistic way of life. Given the circumstance, all else being equal, you may have only the slightest edge over the person you are up against and "everything being equal" is in itself the rarest of the rare. In reality and in point of fact, over time you will be playing a losing game. If you are not on top of your skills, if you are not fiercer and more lethal than the guy you are up against, it's you who will get the parade and be written up in tomorrow's news. At a very real level, you had better be a very good warrior or the time will certainly come when you are the casualty. Know your abilities, know your limitations and play to your strengths. Don't enter a fight you are not, in your mind, heavily favored to win. Okay, you do not always call the shots, but often you do, and in those instances be sure the deck is stacked in your favor, and please, don't give speeches as on television or the movies. Just do what you came there to do and get on with things. There is no tidy, politically correct way to blow someone's head off.

THE
NiGHT
CHICAGO
DiED

Chapter 35

To understand being a cop in Chicago is to understand the city itself. Chicago didn't invent itself in 1966 when I entered the force, nor did it cease in 1988 when I left. There are some things simply greater than its parts and Chicago is one of them.

Due to its position in the country and access by rail and ship, the storied history goes back to when, as the story goes, a cow knocked over a lamp on DeKoven Street and the city burned. The cow never talked and it may have been a setup from the get-go, but that's how the report went down.

Later, Chicago, particularly during prohibition, became the center of the world for illicit fun and mayhem. We all know the story of the Untouchables, of Elliot Ness, of Frank Nitti and, of course, big Al Capone. What would Saint Valentines day be without the massacre? The Tommy gun, rat a tat a tat, cars screaming down State Street and Clark Street, bodies turning up everywhere. Chicago was for all intents and purposes a town dedicated to its vices and what was old is one day new, so perhaps this has not changed. Frank Sinatra loved the city and sung about its allure. Its history was also not easy on the cops. There was the Haymarket Riot where seven men in blue fell. It was a labor protest with the involvement of anarchists and labor demanding the eight-hour work day. A bomb was thrown into the Police Squadron and the party responsible was never identified. The date was May 4, 1886 at Haymarket Square, Randolf Street between Desplaines and Halsted.

This was our history. The underground tunnels and speakeasies that Capone built are still there, as are the old warehouses where beer was made. Turn any corner in old Chicago, open a door, go down the stairs and look under the old carpet and you may yet find gambling chips or a latch that opens into another area entirely. When you put on the uniform you are not just joining the force as you would in Denver, Los Angeles, New York or any of a thousand cities, you are joining the long blue line that goes back into Chicago's and the nations early history, to its most outrageous age. And through those years I was on the force. While Big Al Capone was long gone, the Mob still flourished, still controlled prostitution, numbers, narcotics, gambling, protection and the rest. Bodies were still turning up regularly and gang warfare was never too far off. The new era of electronic surveillance was still years away and to be a Made Member still carried the awesome clout and respect that came with that distinction.

In this chapter I will talk about two men, two alleged associates of the Mob who just recently surfaced to face justice. However, when I knew them they were the movers and shakers, they were untouchable, they were cops. Not just cops, they were high ranking, poster boys for what a tough cop should be. They were royalty, and they were connected.

There are so many stories one can lock into even in the 20 years I worked the streets. I never kowtowed to anyone, not supervisors, politicians, athletes, musicians or actors, and I knew so many of them. Maybe it's because I treated them as I would be treated, that they were friends or, if not friends, then acquaintances. I won't name names, but I knew many of them. I always showed respect where respect was due and some deference when that was called for, but I was always my own man and anyone who did not return that respect could fuck themselves. It's not all that hard to rub shoulders with royalty when the world comes to your doorstep, and that has always been Chicago. If you were looking for mobsters, we had the best.If you were looking for controlling politicians, the best. If crooked cops were your game Chicago was the name. Events that shook the world, like the Manhattan Project, the first atom bomb, worked under the concrete reinforced stadium of the University of Chicago. The '68 Convention, the week that rocked the world, Chicago. To anyone living in the city, then or now, the rest of the world orbits the Windy City, and if you leave, it's only to return. There is a part of Chicago that gets into your bones, your blood and always remains.

It's like the Frank Sinatra's song, "Chicago, Chicago, My Kind of Town." The city keeps getting that new coat of paint, but under it all you can still hear the screeching of tires and the staccato chatter of the .45 cal. Thompsons with 100 round circular magazines, the Chicago Typewriter, cutting down the seven members of the Irish/German gang led by Bugs Moran. The year was 1929 and the South Side Italian gang, or Mob, was led by Al Capone. The North Side Irish/German mob was headed by Bugs Moran. When the only living member of Moran's men was interviewed by the first cops arriving at the garage, he was asked "Who shot you guy?" and his last words were, "Nobody shot me." That's how it was.

By that equation, my time on the force was tame, but the underlying current of violence and vice was always just below the surface, or above the surface and spitting in your face. Today, yesterday's Mob, while still around, is a shadow of its former self, but its place is quickly being taken by the vast number of violent gangs that control the city. Given the choice, I believe Chicagoans and Government would prefer the Mob to the gangs, but then the Mayor today is the son of the Honorable Richard J. Daley, and kids always do it a bit differently. Now to the two Police Officers I knew. What I and others always suspected today turns out to be true: these men in blue were mobbed up.One died and the book will always remain open on him, and the other is in a Federal Penitentiary for his criminal past.

One of these men was a sergeant and in the Family Secrets investigation. The other main player was one of Chicago's most celebrated officer,

Chief of Detectives William Hanhardt. The first man I alluded to died prior to trial and I chose not to disclose his name or speak of his "alleged" crimes. I personally never saw this man do anything illegal, underhanded perhaps, but not illegal, and I only want to speak to what I personally know or what can be supported by court documents.

We have already been introduced to William Hanhardt in the second chapter of this book, only not by name. The staff officer who called in me and the others to mount an offensive to take back the subway system was no other than William Hanhardt. So in a sense, if it were not for William Hanhardt, Superman would have stayed in Metropolis.

If you ever needed to cast the perfect hero in a police drama it would be William Hanhardt. He was a cop's cop and shot his way onto the pages of Chicago's newspapers in the 50s and 60s. He always seemed to know where the next crime was going down and managed to get there first. He had a habit of gunning down the lawless with efficiency, and there were few if any survivors. He was deadly in a calculated way. He always used overwhelming firepower and he was willing to use it without giving it a second thought. The papers just loved him. Later in life, his hair turned a silver white, but he maintained his good looks and was a poster child for what a career cop should be if there ever was one. His fame was not limited to the Chicago PD. He was a paid consultant to Michael Mann's television show, "Crime Story," produced in the 80s.

It was always whispered that he was "connected," but his record was flawless and his success rate unmatched.

Hanhardt served from July 1953 to March 1986 and continues to serve, though now it is in a Federal Penitentiary. He holds the distinction of being the highest ranking Chicago Police Officer ever indicted and convicted on Federal Racketeering, and is serving a 16-year sentence. I will say from my own limited interface with him that he dressed well, was immaculately groomed and spoke softly and with a choice of words above that experienced in the Department. He was a gentlemen and politician. I never had a beef with William Hanhardt.

As I said, it was rumored he was connected for all the years he served and his rise in the ranks was meteoric. His arrest and kill record were legend but his rise was obviously helped by friends in high places with clout. The supposition is that many of his kills and arrests were tips and directly or indirectly tied to Mob business such as failure to pay street tax.

After his retirement from the force in 1986, a marked increase in high-end jewelry burglary and heists were noted in Chicago and many other cities in the western U.S. Authorities in various police Departments and joint task forces marveled at the sophistication and innate understanding of police methods and what was thought to be unique access to information available only to police organizations. Such information would be when gems were being transported, by whom, from point to point and inventories. Also noted would be if armed escort was to be incorporated or if the element of "out of sight out of mind" or "hidden in plain sight" was to be used. The thieves were uncanny in their ability to co-opt the most sophisticated alarm and surveillance systems and vanish without a trace. It was postulated that only a master detective could plan such capers, and in fact a master detective it was. Millions of dollars of gems, jewelry and fine watches were disappearing and authorities were getting no closer. In point of fact, the thieves in their sophistication gave themselves away. They were known to use smoke bombs, aliases, secret codes, bulletproof vests, electronic eavesdropping equipment, costumes and all manner of breaking and entering tools to enact their crimes. This ring flourished for several years before being discovered and disbanded. Hanhardt used the police computers that were being used to track the crimes and it is thought he had inside help from active duty officers. It is an open question whether he was assisted as a favor to a retired favorite son or if others were more deeply involved.

Handhardt was indicted in 2000 and ultimately, in 2002 he pleaded guilty to Federal Racketeering charges.

The other interesting aspect of all this is his supposed tie to the Mob. It is informative that three individuals backed his appointment to the rank of Chief of Detectives: Democratic Committman John

D'Arco Sr. Alderman Fred Roti, and 1st Ward Secretary Pat Marcy. All were known Made Members
of the Mob, or as they are also known, the Chicago
Outfit. It would take an unbelievable amount of na-
ivety not to connect the dots. You may also ask how
that many stolen high- end items could be moved
and again you are left with only one conclusion.
This was a sophisticated operation from beginning
to end.

William Hanhardt is scheduled for release
from Federal Prison in January 2012. There is no
mention in the records of the disposition of over 4.5
million dollars of precious gems, jewelry and other
fine items. To date, he remains the highest ranking
"associate of the Outfit", to be inside the Chicago
Police Department. And I knew him when.

Chapter 36

Writing this book has been good for me, so far at least. Telling my story and showing the dirty laundry was more or less just what I thought it would be. I did my part in relating what happened and trying to put some perspective to those troubled times. I am still the same man who stole and the same one who changed. I am all those people. It has been interesting to put all this down in one place since it unfolded one event at a time.

That's what I don't like about most books, television and films; they all seem to have three parts, beginning, middle and conclusion, and life isn't experienced that way. For me or for anyone, life is one vignette after another, each only loosely connected by some thread that goes through it all. Cop stories seem to resolve themselves in a tidy package with winners, losers and lessons to be learned. For me, again, life just doesn't happen that predictably. Looking back, I see patterns, amazing circumstances, great humor and even greater pathos, but it wasn't planned to happen that way, it just did. My life didn't start when I was 22 years old and didn't end when I was 42, though that is the span of this narration. I went on to other things, Chicago went on as something a little different. The people I knew, those who survived, also went on. Some became politicians, others got their PhDs and write and teach, others just wandered away, but life is like that. If I wanted, I could be very unhappy that my career in law enforcement didn't go better, but then I am able to write this factual account and have something to draw upon. I could remain crushed by the death of my first wife, but life goes on and I have a new life with a new wife today. My children are grown, I am retired, but I have experienced several careers in my time and police work was only one of them.

All in all, I feel rather fortunate to have experienced what I have, to have grown and learned from its lessons and survived some rather turbulent times. As a young man, I let it all hang out and, as an older man who should know better, I still let it hang out. We all, if we live long enough, carry with us things we would prefer to forget and I am no different. I am conscious and in a way respectful of those I killed and hurt but is this any different than a young man who goes to war for his country? I make a rather big point of my convenient lapses in honesty while on the force, but again it was at the time little different in my mind than one little fish swimming in a large school of other little fish. We all do the same thing in much the same way and that in itself feels normal. In retrospect, looking back over the many years and benefiting from the wisdom that age and experience bring, I understand the error of what I did, but would I do it again in exactly the same circumstance... probably. Honestly, it didn't seem all that bad at the time, though that is no excuse nor is it intended to be. I knew, worked with and enjoyed such colorful and diverse personalities, and I doubt I will ever be so fortunate again. Similarly, I experienced so many seminal events that changed history and doubt that situation will recur anytime in my life. Sometimes, it says all that needs to be said, are the words "I was there."

There are two points of satisfaction that I got from doing this book-well, three actually. The first is that my first wife and others, most no longer here, urged me to tell this true story. They felt it had merit and that it says something important. Second, because I can get it all down or at least a progression of events and adventures that represent those 20 years of my life, it becomes a nice chronology. Last, I have finally scratched that damn itch; the one you just can't quite reach, the one that at least from my viewpoint corrects purported history and tells another side to the story. My story is not star-crossed, not particularly heroic, not particularly reinforcing and not entirely damning. It is simply actions and events that I saw and participated in and a description of what went into my eyes, my ears, my nose. I've tried to put you there for the funny, the ridiculous, the ugly, the demeaning, the ironic and the iconic. Yet I didn't write this for you, I did it for myself, for my first wife, for other friends and for anyone interested in real history. If you were entertained, I am pleased. If you were appalled then, well okay. If you heard and read enough to ask some questions and reevaluate those years and what actually happened, then I guess I'd have to say I'm happy.

Know this about me, though. I don't live my life looking back at what was; I still look forward to what will be. There are other stories to tell, but I think I'll just keep them to myself as they are my stories and, believe it or not, I am at my core a private person.

As for Chicago's Other Mob and those who fed off it, the names may have changed and some things look different. Hopefully, we have learned from the past and are trying to correct that which was decayed and dysfunctional. Personally, I think this is wishful thinking and don't believe we have, but again, that is for someone else to investigate and is beyond my personal experience.

Thank you for your time, your indulgence in letting me rant and prattle on and for my occasional bouts with self-personified grandeur.

Believe me when I say I know I was flawed in those days and understand it can be argued I am still the same person and so still flawed, but I would say only one last thing for your studied consideration: if you believe only half of what I say, a third of what I say, then you must believe also that history has done a disservice to Chicago, her leaders, the Police Department (*The Other Chicago Mob*) and to the rank and file. History must not paint this picture or that; history must tell objectively what happened and how that influenced subsequent events. Life is never so tidy that you can wrap it up with a bow and make it look good if it was anything but. This history does not deserve a bow. It deserves dissection, introspection, investigation and above all the truth of what really happen. And isn't it best to do this while some of those who lived and made that history are still among us and perhaps willing to tell the truth?

Anyway, that's how I see it.

10-1: Police officer needs help
10-4: Two-man car
10-99: One-man car
11th and State: Police HQ (Since relocated)
47UART also called a 47: DUI
All Calls: City wide response calls
Arrest: Used instead of collar or take down
Baby Dicks: Youth Officers
Backup: Assist car
Bag man: Moves mob money
Beef: A complaint
Beefer: A complainer
Blow: Breathalyzer
Blue Flu: Police slowdown or work stoppage
Blue Goose: Chrysler with phone in 60s, blue, used by the deputy chiefs
Blue Light Special: Free wild E-ticket ride that ended in the ER
Blues: Police uniform
Brody: A jumper
Bull Dick: Old time station detective who did the formal interrogation
Cage: Car with wired in back seat
CCR: Communications Room, or dispatch
Chase: In hot pursuit
China man: Person of influence
Code 1 or Emergency: Lights and siren response
CR: A complaint register, a formal complaint
Cuffs: Handcuffs
Dicks: Detectives
DOA: Any dead person

Downer: Drunk on the ground or ill person
Dress Blues: Special occasion uniform
Drop gun or knife: Plant, just in case
Enforcer: Mob guy
ET: Evidence Technician
Five-O: Undercover cops
Flipped Over: When you took the governors off
the engine which controlled maximum speed
Floater: A dead body in the lake
Freebie: Anything that you don't pay for
Full Boat: No discount
Full Float: Flat bed truck, tow
Ghetto District: Primarily African-American
District
Going to the west side: Cook County jail and
court houses were on the west side
Hit the Bricks: Hit the street, to start a day
Hit the medical: Home sick
Hook: Tow Truck
Hot or Cold: Wants and warrants or plates
IAD: Internal Affairs Division
In Progress: Any hot call
In the bag: Caught, cornered, the jig is up
IOD: Injured on duty
Irish: Turkeys
Italians: Grease balls or dagoes
Jews: Sheenies or Hebes
Johnny: As in "Johnny Law," cop
Latinos: Spics, Beaners
Lockup: Jail
Made or Made Member: Full fledged mobster in

the Mafia

Mars Lights: All emergency vehicles in Chicago use flashing blue lights

Mars Lights: Bubble gum machines, blue on roof

Maxwell St: Vice Unit location

Mickey the Mope: Average citizen or fuckup.

Miscellaneous Reporting guide: Alpha numeric system for shorthand reporting and reports

Mopes: citizen

Motherfucker: Motherfucker

Motor Pool: Towed Vehicles

On View: Witnessed while on patrol

OPS: Office of Professional Standards, a civilian oversight commission

OT: Overtime or pay

Piece: Gun

Plainclothes: Civilian dress

Polish: Pollock

Pool Car: Barely running piece of shit with 200K miles on it

Pronged: When you got fucked by someone, usually your boss

Red Line: If you failed to respond after three pages you were cited, very serious

Reefer: Large wool overcoat

Righteous Shooting: A good, justified shooting

Rod: Gun

Rosco: Gun

SAP: A leather case over lead balls or sand used to smash someone

Sgt. Ward: Inspector in the district

Shit house: Jail
Shit Kicker: Appalachian
Siren or warble woop: Various siren sounds were used so responding emergency vehicles could hear each other and not cancel each other out.
Slammer: Jail
Slow Down: Tell other cars to back off when you reach the scene and access the situation
Snitch: A stool pigeon, someone who sells information (or trades it)
SO: Special Operations
SOL: Shit out of luck
Squadrol: Paddy Wagon
Stand-up guy: A guy who plays by the rules, not the police rules, but the rules set by the other officers
Star and Shield: Badge on you uniform, shield on your hat
Stinker: Really dead person
TF: Task Force
The Lake: Lake Michigan, one of the Great Lakes
Three Wheelers: Three wheel motorcycles
Time Due: Prior to the union there was no overtime compensation
Time Due: After the union was in place
Tough guy: A guy, cop, civilian or hard-nosed crook who asks no quarter, gives no quarter
Trick bag: Really fucked up and in trouble
Trimming: Beat the fuck out of someone
Trunk job: Dead body in the trunk or one that is

about to be, a Mob term
Uniforms: White hats for traffic, blue for patrol;
(everything os blue today)
Up or Down: Up you are in service, down you
are off service.
VCD: Vice Control Division
White Hats: Traffic cops
Ziegler Box: Metal sealed box for stinkers or
leakers; a coffin

EPILOGUE

I look back at my life as a cop I did things I am not proud of, wrong things, criminal things. What I didn't say is that there were those instances when with the benefit of hindsight I wish I had exacted that last ounce of violence. What haunts me to this very day are some I misread and let pass, who subsequently murdered and did unspeakable crimes against the most innocent. The infamous I-57 killers were known for using a shotgun to get sexual pleasure from the torture and killing of young innocent women and men. The world would be simply better off without some people being here.

This book has set the stage for our forthcoming book *The Other Chicago Mob, Street Stories.*

The Other Chicago Mob: The True Story of Gary Cohen Man in Blue has opened the floodgates and people are already coming forth with their take on those days. We will take you deeper than anyone has been before. You will read firsthand stories that tell about a city that works during the day, but once the sun goes down, the scum will come out. The thin blue line is all that stands between the good people and the crooks and lowlifes. You may not like how the job was done, but think of the alternative.

In the milieu we write about, even with the passaging of time not much has changed. The names are pretty much the same, and who protects the innocent... sometimes not even the cop in a patrol car or one walking a beat!!!!

ACKNOWLEDGEMENTS

I would like to thank the following people for their help, insight and assistance in the writing and preparation of this book.

Thanks first to Gary Cohen who had the faith in me to tell his story.

Ralph Grills, my business partner and friend.

Victor Tsai , for his quiet competence and willingness to take on any task.

Atlas Press, our Distributor and mentor.

Mr. Leon Decker and Bill Todtz for providing research for the book.

To my family for their many years of encouragement and emphasis on the arts, both visual and written.

Thank you all,

Verne Elliot Glassman

Ps: Illustrations/cover art by Verne Elliot Glassman

EXHIBITS

Exhibit A

Gary aged 24

Exhibit B

(Left Photo) Gary - with unknown Federal Agent
(Center Top Photo) Gary - at Police H.Q. standing by
statue honoring Officers at the Hay Market Riots
(Right Photo) Gary - Working Undercover
(Bottom Photo) Police Vehicles near Wrigley Field

Exhibit C

HandBook - Issued to all Police Officers, containing
relevent information

Exhibit D

Tools of the trade!

Exhibit E

Certificate from Orlando W. Wilson

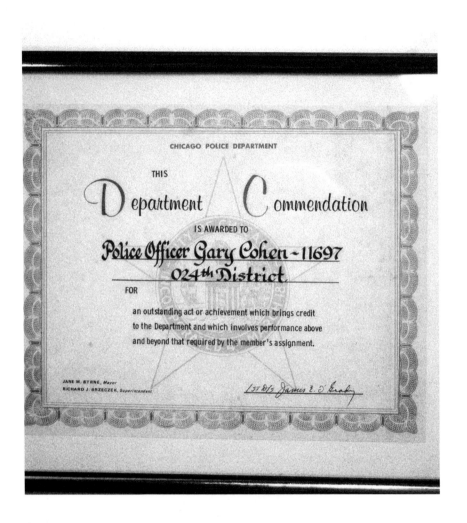

Exhibit F

One of several awards Gary received during his career

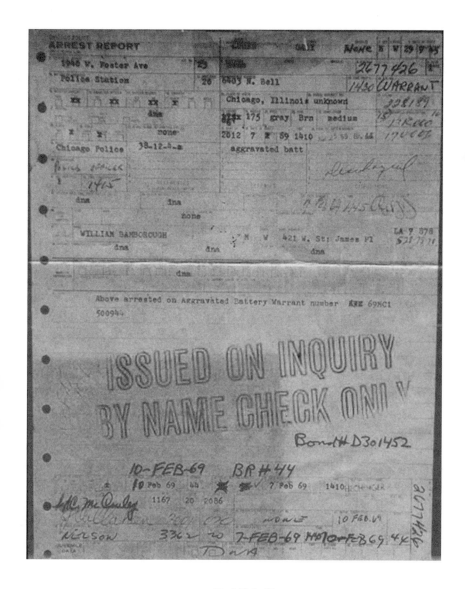

Exhibit G

Gary's arrest report.

Exhibit H

Gary's first wife, Bonita (Aspen Colorado)

Exhibit I

Gary and his current wife, Maria in Mexico

Exhibit J

Gary's girls, Britt and Randi

About the Author

Verne Elliot Glassman has lived a dual life in the arts and the sciences. He worked in aerospace on the Space Shuttle, Star Wars and related projects for over 30 years. He is also a published artist, photographer and writer.

His interests are wide and varied. He has experienced more in his life then the average ten people might but still considers himself always the student. Verne has a formal education is in architecture, art history, and anthropology with advanced studies in business. His life is rich in unique experience and adventure and one thing can be said of Verne, he takes the road less traveled.

Verne considers himself a generalist with considerable experience and knowledge in many areas but not one exclusively. As a man with one foot in the technical world and the other in aesthetics he bridges the gap and takes from both that which is most relevant.

See more about Verne at www.gepub.com